Environmental Education

Benjamin Aldrich-Moodie

and

Jo Kwong

D1614560

Published by
The IEA Education and Training Unit
and the IEA Environment Unit, 1997

First published in September 1997 by
The Education and Training Unit and
The Environment Unit
The Institute of Economic Affairs
2 Lord North Street
Westminster
London SW1P 3LB

Many IEA publications are translated into languages
other than English or are reprinted. Permission to
translate or to reprint should be sought from the
Editorial Director at the address above.

Printed in Great Britain by
Hartington Fine Arts Limited, Lancing, West Sussex
Set in Times Roman and Univers

Contents

3

4

An American Perspective on Environmental Literacy: A New Goal For Environmental Education

Dr Jo Kwong

Foreword

Some time in the early 1970s, in a geography class at school, I took on the project in a class debate of opposing the Third London Airport then planned for the Maplin Sands in Essex. I was fiercely green on the subject and I really did not see why a rare bird, the Brent goose, should go extinct to make way for aeroplanes. Although eventually the argument went my way on the national stage, I lost the school debate by a large margin, my affection for rare geese a subject of some mirth to my colleagues.

The experience was valuable in two ways. First, it taught me to question my own assumptions: it had not crossed my mind that some people might not see the (to me) self-evident importance of protecting rare geese. Second, I remember the teacher taking a strictly neutral position on the matter. He did not try to make up our minds for us but he tried to help us make up our own minds.

Anecdotal reports have filtered through to my adult ears since then of what children are now taught about environmental issues in school, but it was not until I read the essays by Benjamin Aldrich-Moodie and Dr Jo Kwong that I realised how bad things have got. Their quotations from school textbooks make chilling reading. It appears that in place of education, children are frequently subjected to propaganda, leading questions and plain errors of fact. Instead of being given the science they are handed opinions and told to regurgitate them in letters to politicians. Instead of being urged to think for themselves they are being taught settled conclusions: the world is being destroyed; economic growth and new technology are to blame.

Yet when I think of the biggest environmental debates of the past twenty years, I can think of only one in which those environmentalists who hold to this view have been right: the effect of DDT on birds of prey. Every other scare was false: the world was going to freeze; pesticides were becoming more poisonous; acid rain was the cause of forest decline; oil would run out by the end of the century; per-capita food production would fall in the 1980s and 1990s resulting in widespread famine; per-capita energy use would increase; population growth would accelerate; renewable energy would do less environmental damage than fossil fuels; the Sahara desert would expand; new industries would be more polluting than old ones; free trade would be bad for the environment; banning the trade in rhino horn would save rhinos whereas allowing the trade in crocodile skins would threaten crocodiles; rain forest loss would prove irreversible; oil spills would have long-term effects on marine life. The list of wrong predictions goes on and on.

Of course, although I can make a very strong case that each of the above predictions was wrong, many of the old school of environmentalists would challenge me on them; and the jury is still out on others, notably global warming and the 'hole' in the ozone layer. But that is exactly the point: these issues are debatable and debated they should be. Is wind energy really greener than fossil-fuels when it requires large acreages of moorland to be covered in ugly steel towers serviced by bulldozed roads? What a wonderful topic for children to debate, with no preconceived 'right' answer, because there is none. Or, to take another example from Jo Kwong's essay, one question in a test for school children asked them to circle the picture that best answered the question 'Which way do people endanger animals?'. The 'right' answer is the picture of a logging machine. But surely a strong case could be made that the girl petting a cat is the greater danger to wildlife, given the number of birds killed by domestic cats. There is no 'right' answer to such questions.

It is not only mind-narrowing to tell school children the 'answers' rather than to encourage them to ask questions, it is also dull. As Dr Kwong argues in her essay, the version of environmental 'science' presented in most school textbooks is a counsel of despair, unrelieved by a sense of excitement at learning how the world works. It seems designed purely to use children as agents in making their parents feel guilty, a disgraceful form of exploitation of educational opportunity. Luckily, I suspect most children are highly resistant to propagandising of any kind. But this is little consolation when you think of the missed opportunities it represents to teach them science instead of advocacy.

Criticism is easy when teaching has been so perverted by special interests. But could it really be done better? The critic has a duty to demonstrate that it could. This is where Benjamin Aldrich-Moodie's essay is so valuable, because he gives clear and well-written examples of what good textbooks could say about certain environmental issues. These not only shame the existing textbooks with their open-mindedness, but they are also much more exciting to read. Above all, they invite the reader into the debate by presenting the unknowns as well as the knowns.

The distortions, exaggerations and biases so evident in many school textbooks on environmental science seem to indicate an underlying lack of confidence among the environmentalists whose views they reflect. If their case is a strong one, they have nothing to fear from telling the truth and presenting both sides of the argument. The sooner we move away from indoctrination, and replace it with education, the better.

June 1997   DR MATT RIDLEY
Columnist, The Daily Telegraph and Author

Dr Ridley is the author of *The Origins of Virtue* and *The Red Queen*, both of which were short-listed for the Rhone-Poulenc Science Book Prize. The IEA has published two collections of Dr Ridley's newspaper columns and articles, and he is a Fellow of the IEA Environment Unit.

The Authors

Benjamin Aldrich-Moodie is beginning a PhD in Politics at Princeton University. He completed his BA in History at Yale University where he wrote a thesis on proletarian satire in early 20th century Russia, and received an MPhil in Social and Political Theory at Cambridge University after writing on George Herbert Mead's social psychology and the crisis of the state in contemporary Russia. He also completed the Diploma in Economics at Cambridge. In the summer and autumn of 1996 he worked at the IEA researching and writing the current publication (his first).

Dr Jo Kwong is the Environmental Research Associate at the Atlas Economic Research Foundation in Fairfax, VA, and a research professor at George Mason University. By appointment of the Governor of Virginia, she serves on the State Water Control Board and on the Virginia Conservation and Recreation Foundation. Kwong received her doctorate from the University of Michigan's School of Natural Resources at Ann Arbor, Michigan, and her BA in biology from Brown University in Providence, RI.

Kwong has written several books on environmentalism, including *Myths about Environmental Policy* (Citizens for the Environment, Washington, DC), *Protecting the Environment: Old Rhetoric, New Imperatives* (Capital Research Center, Washington, DC), and *Market Environmentalism: Lessons for Hong Kong* (Hong Kong Centre for Economic Research). She is a contributing author to *The Yellowstone Primer: Land and Resource Management in the Greater Yellowstone Ecosystem* (Pacific Research Institute for Public Policy, San Francisco) and *Rational Readings on Environmental Concerns* (Van Nostrand Reinhold, New York). In addition, Kwong has published in many journals including the *Harvard Journal of Law and Public Policy*, *Urban Lands* and the *American Land Forum*, as well as in the popular press such as the *Wall Street Journal* and *The New York Times*.

Kwong lectures on environmentalism in the United States and around the world. Her recent research areas include eco-theology, or the religion of environmentalism; and environmental education. In her work at the Atlas Economic Research Foundation, she encourages and supports public policy institutes that teach people about free market environmentalism.

Acknowledgements

For help in coming to terms with some of the science behind the acid rain and global warming issues, I must particularly thank Gwyneth Howells of Cambridge University and Beth Newell of Hobart College in Geneva, New York. Any faults that remain in my discussion of these topics are my own. At the IEA, I thank Julian Morris, who found me sources, gave editorial comment, and was a good arguing partner, James Tooley who reviewed my writing, nudged me along, and arranged for me to meet teachers, and Lisa Mac Lellan, who helped co-ordinate the project. Susan Whitfield advised me as to the workings of the English education system. Dr Ashley Kent and Dr David Lambert of the Institute of Education's Centre for Education, Environment and Economy gave me helpful advice and allowed me to meet teachers on their MA course – I'd like to thank all of these teachers for valuable discussion, and especially Maree Connoley, who showed me the materials she uses in her classroom and some of her students' work. Finally, I wish to thank Dunbar Moodie for his comments on a draft of the manuscript and, last but not least, Felicity Ussher, whose editorial advice was always exact and affectionate.

B. A.-M.

Many thanks to Alejandro Chafuen, president of the Atlas Economic Research Foundation, for sharing episodes from the popular American cartoon, Captain Planet, with me. The show's attacks on entrepreneurs, scientists and people in general propelled my research into the area of environmental education. A special thanks also goes to Ken Chilton and his staff at the Center for the Study of American Business in St Louis, Missouri, for their support and editing of the publication on which this article is based.

J. K.

Environmental Education: A Study of Texts

Benjamin Aldrich-Moodie

Introduction

This study of environmental education in England was commissioned by the Institute of Economic Affairs out of a concern that children are not receiving an adequate account of the debate over environmental issues. In her companion essay on environmental education in America, Jo Kwong criticises US environmental education for teaching advocacy rather than knowledge. By contrast, this paper focuses on the texts which are used in environmental education in the UK.

Sources

Environmental education in England is a vast enough enterprise that a brief study such as this must be modest in its choice of sources. In my research, I draw primarily on textbook discussions of environmental issues from the Key Stage 2 to GCSE level. I have tried to find the most up-to-date textbooks available in the British Library, and have made an effort to include only those which are clearly selling well, and are thus most representative. Some GCSE exam questions (from the London board) and teaching material published by environmental organisations also make a showing in the analysis.

This choice of sources necessarily excludes any account of the way teachers modify and adapt (or perhaps ignore) the textbooks, although I have talked with some teachers about the way they conduct environmental education. It also misses some of the evidently thriving aspects of British environmental education outside the classroom. These include the use of the out-of-doors for science studies and landscaping projects that involve pupils in the improvement of school grounds as areas to play and observe nature. Another extra-curricular source of environmental education worth mentioning is the Groundwork programme, which among other things links schools and industries to share thoughts about the practical business of working toward environmental quality.

Contents and Analytical Approach

Within the domain of school and exam texts, I have chosen to concentrate on five topics which recur frequently and seem to be particularly rich with opportunities for constructive criticism. In other words, while this study does contain some praise for selected passages from environmental education texts, its intent is primarily critical. In the initial chapter, I examine the way in which the dichotomy between renewable and non-renewable resources currently obscures an adequate rendition of the economics of resource use in the science and geography curriculum. The next chapter is devoted to an exploration of the gap between academic knowledge and schoolbook science in the presentation of the highly complex issue of acid rain. In Chapter 3, I look at global warming and the way scientific uncertainty about the issue is dealt with in textbook accounts. In Chapter 4, I examine the way 'desertification' is dealt with in the curriculum. Finally, I take a brief look at the strengths and weaknesses of textbook accounts of conservation.

There are two main strains of criticism I make in the following pages. One is that the discussion of these issues in educational texts is frequently inaccurate or lopsided. The other is that the use of statistics and other evidence to support these discussions is often fraught with internal contradictions or inaccuracies. Important questions that would be raised by a serious and close analysis of the evidence presented go unanswered and unnoticed by the authors. This last failing is particularly unfortunate, since it indicates that children are missing the crucial and difficult lesson of how to approach evidence with an inquiring scepticism that both probes it for weaknesses and searches out its implications. Just as important as providing children with a 'balanced' account of the environmental debate is an effort to prepare them as best as possible to take part critically and constructively in that debate.

Researching these environmental issues has given me a healthy respect for the difficulties faced by teachers trying to make out a balanced account of current knowledge for their pupils. While the standard popular presentation of environmental issues is often flawed, books put out for the general reader which claim to debunk environmental myths frequently suffer from the opposite bias. I have tried to seek out sources about these issues that seem to me to represent as closely as possible authoritative academic thinking on the subject. Some of the issues are still the centre of lively academic dispute where it is quite difficult to locate a solid centre ground; this is true particularly of the global warming debate, but even there I think it is possible to deliver a more balanced representation of the central issues than is obtainable in most texts readily available to teachers and pupils. I also include a rough model textbook passage to furnish a concrete example of how the complexities of each environmental issue in question might be more fully presented in a GCSE-level text.

1. Renewable and Non-Renewable Resources

The National Curriculum programme of study provides amply for the discussion of resource use. By the end of Key Stage 2 (ages 7-11), the 'physical processes' division of the Science curriculum requires that pupils 'understand the difference between renewable and non-renewable energy resources and the need for fuel economy' (DES, 1991b, p. 13). In Geography, pupils of the same age learn to 'distinguish between renewable and non-renewable resources' (DES, 1991a, p. 26). This in and of itself is hardly objectionable; some resources do indeed reproduce themselves while others do not, and, of course, needless waste of resources is always deplorable.

The Mother Hubbard Theory of Resources

Unfortunately, the way in which school textbooks develop these themes is often highly misleading and misinformed. The discussion of non-renewable resources often rests on the assumption that the earth contains a limited and well-defined basket of useful materials. Once this perspective is established, it is easy to come to the conclusion that people are quickly consuming the earth's non-renewable resources, and that, once used, they are exhausted once and for all. One day in the not-too-distant future, humanity will wake up to find that the cupboard is bare.

This line of argument is not new, and has been the source of consistently false predictions of resource exhaustion for some time. For instance, a famous 1972 report called *The Limits to Growth* predicted that 'the world would run out of gold by 1981, mercury by 1985, tin by 1987, zinc by 1990, petroleum by 1992, and copper, lead, and natural gas by 1993' (cited in East *et al.*, 1994, p. 121). Many geography and science texts which discuss resource reserves (usually in the context of energy sources) make the same sorts of predictions as the ones made in *The Limits to Growth* report. The forecasts are updated, of course, like the

16

steep drop at the edge of the Earth that is always just on the horizon. But the misconceptions that generate them are the same.

This is perhaps best illustrated in an example from the Oxford University Press's *Access to Geography 3*. The book has a section entitled 'When the oil runs out' that begins: 'In August 1989, the USA announced it only had twelve years supply of oil left' (Kemp *et al.*, 1992, p. 90). It is difficult to divine what the statement means (or, indeed, precisely who made it). My guess would be that it was made on the following basis: in 1989, known reserves of oil within US territory that were exploitable at contemporary prices matched the country's projected consumption over the course of the next 12 years. Even if true, this in no way means that petrol pumps will run dry in August 2001 in the US, although this is evidently the impression that the authors of *Access to Geography* intend to convey, given that they move from the US 'announcement', without further comment, into a discussion of solar, wind, geothermal, and wave-based power generation.

An Economic Theory of Resources

The reason why petrol stations will not suddenly close up shop in 2001, or, for that matter, in 2020 or 2040 as another textbook suggests (Johnson *et al.*, 1995b, p. 19), has to do with the economics of non-renewable resource use. Children should be taught that the 'problem' of energy reserves (or of any other non-renewable resource) is essentially about the price of energy sources. A substance like oil will never 'run out' suddenly at a future date. Rather, its price will rise steadily as reserves are depleted. To some extent, this price rise is checked by the fact that it stimulates a search for new reserves, makes more diffuse sources economically exploitable, and gives producers the incentive to squeeze more out of old wells, thereby boosting supplies. This sort of process has contributed to the more than sevenfold increase in proven world-wide reserves of oil and gas from 1950 to 1990 (Moore, 1995, p. 116). Rising prices not only help to expand reserves; they also give consumers an incentive to economise on consumption, and intensify the search for substitutes. Many of the 'alternative energy sources' mentioned by textbook authors are not worth developing presently because

17

they are so costly. They will become economical only once the price of energy rises above the cost of their production.

All too many textbook authors miss this point entirely. The authors of *Access to Geography 3* recognise that 'the low price of oil' is among the reasons for the slow development of renewable energy resources. While this makes perfect economic sense for the reasons discussed above, against the background of the earlier statement that the USA has announced it will run out of oil in the year 2001, it leaves the reader with the impression that low oil prices are blinding the international community to the coming energy crisis. In fact, low prices indicate the market's collective view that oil supplies will be fairly abundant relative to demand for some time to come. One London-based GCSE exam question also misses the connection between prices and resource availability. It shows a graph of 'proved world fossil fuel resources in 1990' (Figure 1) which gives coal 226 years, natural gas 59 years, and oil 33 years 'before [the] resources expire'. Readers are first asked to '[e]xplain what is likely to happen to world prices of fossil fuels' (University of London Examinations and Assessment Council, 1992, p. 6), but evidently the examiners have no conception of how the expected rise in fossil fuel prices call into question the validity of their graph. In keeping with textbook convention the examiners next ask readers about the 'alternative' energies available. To their credit, the question asks for an assessment of the environmental impact of the different 'alternatives', but overall the examiners require (and display) little comprehension of the economics of energy use.

The authors of the Geography Project texts also portray renewable sources as the only hope in a coming age of energy scarcity. They title their section on energy in the *Developed World* volume 'The Power Crisis – On The Edge Of Darkness' (Punnett *et al.*, 1988, p. 68). Rather than listing the usual series of expiry dates for the different fossil fuels, the authors conduct a lengthy discussion of the Chernobyl disaster, then come to the following judgements about contemporary sources of electricity: 'many people think that nuclear power is too dangerous to be a good source of energy. Oil is too precious to burn for power

18

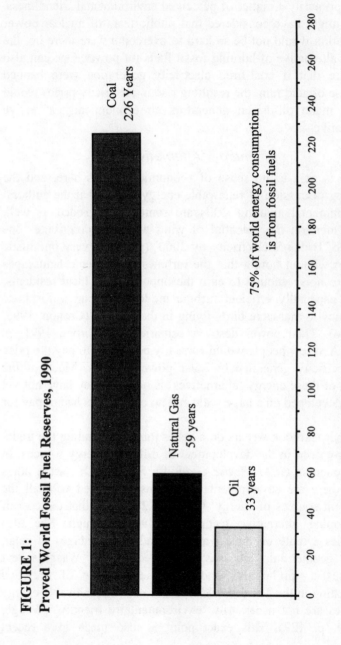

FIGURE 1:
Proved World Fossil Fuel Reserves, 1990

Coal
226 Years

Natural Gas
59 years

Oil
33 years

75% of world energy consumption
is from fossil fuels

Source: London Examinations, a division of the Edexcel Foundation, GCSE,
Thursday 9 June 1992, Geography [Syllabus A] 3E: Energy (Optional Paper), p. 6.

generation. Coal-fired power stations cause acid rain.' (pp. 68-69). These authors seem to consider the choice of energy sources to be primarily a matter of perceived environmental friendliness. They might have considered that public fears of nuclear power generation would not be so hard to overcome were there not the cheap alternative of burning fossil fuels for power. One can also be sure that if coal-fired electricity generation were banned because of acid rain, the resulting rise in electricity prices would likely make oil-driven generators an economically attractive alternative.

Energy 'Alternatives'

There is next to no sense of economic realities here, and the ensuing discussion of renewable energy shows that the authors' environmental auditing skills are somewhat lopsided as well. They mention the potential of wind power to contribute 'one tenth of Britain's electricity by 2000' (p. 69) (a very optimistic figure) without noting that the turbines spoil scenic landscapes and are noisy enough to earn the opposition of local residents; some especially efficient turbine models have an unfortunate tendency to massacre birds flying in the vicinity (Cronon, 1995, p. 226). Tidal power destroys estuaries (Cairncross, 1991, p. 107). And few people would currently be willing to pay the price of electricity generated by solar power stations. Much of the allure of these energy 'alternatives' is because they have not yet been developed on a large scale and no one has yet had to pay for them.

Other textbook writers do a better job of illustrating the trade-offs involved in the development of different energy sources. In the Longman *GCSE Revise Guide* for Science, Di Barton notes that 'there are environmental problems associated with all the different sources of energy' (1993, p. 281), and that the cost of developing alternative technologies is very high. She also supplies a table on the advantages and disadvantages of solar, tidal, geothermal, and wave-generated power. Waugh's text features a similar list, and uses the example of firewood harvesting in the Third World to illustrate why renewable energy sources are not necessarily 'environmentally friendly' (Waugh, 1994a, p. 129). This exact point is also made in a recent

Geography GCSE exam (1995b, p. 11).[1] So there are signs of an increasing realisation in the educational literature that the renewable/non-renewable dichotomy obscures as much as it reveals when it comes to judging the problems surrounding resource use.

Conservation

The textbook focus on 'developing' renewable energy tends to overlook one of the most environmentally-friendly and economically important ways of dealing with scarce energy sources – conservation. The National Curriculum Science requirements mention the 'need for fuel economy' (DES, 1991b, p. 13), but their emphasis on the difference between renewable and non-renewable resources may well distract attention from the importance of energy conservation. After all, if oil is truly set to run out suddenly in 33 years, economising on consumption will do no more than put off the fateful day, perhaps until 50-odd years in the future. Even with this revised deadline, the most important priority would be to have 'alternative' energy sources up and running when the last drop of oil is burnt. In fact, given that the increasing scarcity of non-renewable resources is a much more gradual phenomenon, energy conservation, rather than the exploitation of 'alternative' energy sources, will prove to be the cheapest response to gradually rising fuel prices for a very long time to come. History shows that there is plenty of room for improving energy efficiency when economic necessity bites. In response to upward shocks in the price of oil, per capita energy use in the OECD countries fell by 6 per cent from 1973-85, while the same economies grew by 24 per cent (Cairncross, 1995, p. 125).[2] Further substantial gains in efficiency are no doubt

---

[1] Although see Leach and Mearns (1996, p. 2), for a discussion of the problems with the idea of a 'woodfuel crisis' in Africa.

[2] Even without the sudden imperative of a price shock, the cost of energy exerts a steady impetus towards greater efficiency. So, over time, steel producers have made their product using less and less energy, soft-drink manufacturers have thinned the walls of aluminium cans to save on the large amounts of electricity needed to produce aluminium metal, car manufacturers have made increasingly efficient internal-combustion engines, and so on.

possible, even simply by applying currently available technologies.

There is a running debate as to whether some of the conservation technologies currently available are not applied more universally because they are too expensive for the savings they deliver at current energy prices, or because there are significant shortcomings in the market that slow down their implementation. Most economists resist the argument that people under-invest in conservation because of a lack of information or simple myopia; it runs against their assumption that market actors are 'rational' and that they will search out information that is truly important to their economic decisions. In the face of studies showing that people demand an irrationally high rate of return from energy-saving investments (Cairncross, 1991, p. 115), they might point out that some energy-saving devices are not more popular with consumers because of qualitative problems with their performance. For instance, super-efficient light bulbs sometimes illuminate slowly, and the light they give off can be harsh, akin to that given off by overhead fluorescent tubes. Learning about the pros and cons of different energy-saving opportunities at school may be a good way of promoting sensible energy conservation while honing more basic intellectual skills like mathematics. A Groundwork project called Esso Young Energy Savers is an example of an educational project designed to promote conservation through 'a dual energy education and energy saving program for primary schools'.[3] Whatever the details of the approach educators take to teaching energy conservation, they should point out that sensible energy conservation is about making good investments, not about desperately postponing the day when non-renewable energy sources will come to an end. Energy-saving measures that cost more than they can deliver are best not implemented. The money could be better spent elsewhere, say on buying up threatened wildlife habitat. Good teaching about non-renewable resource use is an opportunity to show how being environmentally

---

[3] Information about this project can be obtained by writing to Barry Watson at Groundwork Colne Valley, Colne Valley Park Centre, Denham Court Drive, Denham, Uxbridge, Middlesex UB9 5PG.

responsible and being smart with money can come to the same thing.

An Alternative Textbook Passage

Some natural resources, such as plants and animals, replace themselves, and so are called 'renewable resources'. Others do not, or are generated very slowly. These are called 'non-renewable resources'. The fossil fuels which we rely on to drive our cars, heat our homes, and generate much of our electricity, are non-renewable in this sense.

The term 'non-renewable' makes it seem as if a resource like oil is a bit like soda in a bottle; some day all of our cars and water-heaters and power plants will simply drink up the last drop. Actually, this is not really right. It is a bit of a trick played on us by the term 'non-renewable'. To understand why something like oil will never be used up to the last drop, you need to have a look at what happens to the price of any non-renewable resource as it gets consumed.

A substance like oil will never 'run out' suddenly at a future date. Rather, its price will rise steadily as supplies of it are depleted. To some extent, this rise in prices is slowed down by the fact that it stimulates a search for new reserves. Business people will make more risky and more costly searches for new supplies of oil as its value goes up. Rising prices also make it worthwhile to extract more spread-out and costly sources, thereby boosting supplies. This sort of process has contributed to the more than sevenfold increase in proven world-wide reserves of oil and gas from 1950 to 1990.

In addition, as prices rise, the people buying the oil have reason to economise on consumption. When agreements between Arab oil producers caused oil prices to rise in the 1970s, people switched to smaller, more fuel-efficient cars. Rising prices for a non-renewable resource also increase the search for substitutes for it. An expensive process to convert plentiful coal to oil will become affordable only after supplies of crude oil in the ground become sufficiently expensive. Long before the last drop of oil is taken out of the ground, it will have been abandoned for other energy sources which are more affordable.

Other renewable energy sources have been proposed as alternatives to fossil fuels. Sometimes these are called 'alternative' energy sources. They include solar, wave, tidal, wind, and geothermal power. One of the main reasons these are not used on a wide scale is that they tend to be more expensive than fossil fuels. While all of these sources have the virtue of not producing pollution, they have other limitations. Since power cannot be stored very efficiently, sources like solar and wind generators cannot be relied upon to produce electricity precisely when people need it the most. Wave power has a lot of technological problems to overcome. Tidal power generators harm river estuary habitats, and wind turbines can be noisy and unsightly. No source of power is trouble-free.

One of the best responses to rising energy prices is to invest in technologies that save on energy use. By applying currently available technologies, people could conserve a lot of the electricity they use now. However, some of these technologies are quite expensive and will not be worth buying until the price of energy goes up.

2. Acid Rain

The problem of acid rain is already a somewhat old-fashioned member of the rapidly developing canon of environmental concerns. It was not long ago, however, that the issue occupied centre stage among public worries about the environment. Acid rain was first raised internationally as an environmental issue in a Swedish report to the United Nations in 1972. The report helped prompt the beginning of state-sponsored research into acid precipitation in the US, Canada, Germany and Norway. Much of this initial work focused on the impact of acidic deposition on crops and aquatic ecosystems. However, in 1984, when there were reports of widespread forest decline on both sides of the Atlantic, scientists began examining the effects of the pollutant on forests as well (NAPAP, 1990, pp. 18-26 to 18-27). For a time, public attention was riveted on acid rain.

Today, forest decline in Europe has stabilised or even reversed itself (Howells, 1995, p. 70), and acid rain is no longer the white-hot environmental disaster story it was. While environmentalists have not forgotten about acid rain, their energies tend to be focused elsewhere. Meanwhile, over the course of the past decade, a good deal of scientific work has been and continues to be done to investigate the causes and effects of acidification in the environment. In school textbook descriptions of acid rain, however (and, I would imagine, in most non-academic presentations of the problem), the results of this research are usually overlooked. It seems that the full litany of fears voiced about acid rain during the mid-1980s has crystallised into a canonical account of the problem, one that persists despite its divergences from contemporary scientific thinking.

One of the mainstays of the schoolbook presentation of the issue goes back to the days of its linkage to forest dieback in Europe and America. A diagram featured in the *Access to Geography 3* text purports to show the effect of acid rain on trees through 'direct damage to needles, leaves, and bark' and root damage through soil acidification (Kemp *et al.*, 1995, p. 30).

Another geography textbook takes a simpler approach, featuring newspaper headlines announcing: 'Acid rain killing trees and birds, warns new report,' 'British conifers most polluted' (Marsden and Marsden, 1995, p. 29). In *The Green Umbrella*, a WWF source book for environmental assemblies, the chapter on the air contains the 'fact' that '[o]ver half of Germany's forests are dead or dying. Most scientists say this is because of acid rain' (WWF, 1991, p. 25). The Longman GCSE Revise Guide for Biology states that '[a]cid rain has been widely attributed to be the cause of forest "dieback" (large-scale death or poor growth of trees) in North America and in Europe' (Barker *et al.*, 1994, p. 292). The authors of *Spotlight Science* claim that '[e]vidence is growing of links between acid rain and a number of serious environmental problems including damage to trees, especially conifers [and] increased plant disease' (Johnson *et al.*, 1995b, p. 54). This adds up to quite a consensus.

Scientific Evidence

In reality, evidence has been growing for a more complex linkage between acid rain and damage to plants than the one nearly unanimously reported in textbooks. Acid rain is not the acute cause of plant death it was once feared to be. The National Acid Precipitation Assessment Program (NAPAP), a half-billion-dollar study funded by the US government and concluded in 1990, reported that '[t]he popular notion that forests throughout the United States and Canada are in a state of decline due to "acid rain" is contradicted by available scientific information' (pp. 16-145). In fact, acid rain has been shown in the first instance to act as something of a tree fertiliser:

'A wide range of field studies involving irrigation of seedling and sapling trees with simulated acid rain in both Scandinavia and the United States have typically produced growth stimulation attributed to the fertiliser effect of the [sulphur and nitrogen] in the irrigant' (pp. 18-69).

For North American forests as a whole, NAPAP concluded that

'[a]cidic deposition has not been shown to be a significant factor contributing to current forest health problems, with the possible

26

exception of spruce die-back and mortality at high elevations in the northern Appalachians' (pp. 16-145).

The only trees adversely affected by acid rain belong to one species at the high-altitude fringes of their range, whose susceptibility to cold damage appears to be enhanced by their exposure to acidic fog. This hardly adds up to massive acidity-induced forest dieback in North America.

Research into forest decline in Europe has come up with similar findings. As the resident expert on acid rain at Cambridge University explains: '[f]orest decline takes a variety of forms and is not a specific disease with a single cause. Climatic changes can explain their temporal coincidence in Europe' (Howells, 1995, p. 219). There is a possibility that acid rain has contributed significantly to magnesium leaching in some forest stands poor in the mineral, but '[f]orest response to magnesium deficiency, possibly enhanced by soil acidification, also reflects intensive forestry practice and can be reversed by appropriate fertilisation regimes' (*ibid.*, p. 70). Acid rain, in this context, appears as a factor that can exacerbate the environmental stresses of high-yield modern forestry.

While test after test has shown acid rain at prevalent levels not to be a significant cause of plant damage in the short term, some evidence is emerging that points towards longer-term deleterious effects to plant growth. It seems that chronic soakings in acidified rain can alter nutrient cycles in forest ecosystems and lead to reduced plant productivity in those environments. While acid rain is not the grim reaper of the forest that it has often been made out to be, it does exert long-term stresses on sylvian eco-systems.

The effects of acid rain on crops, however, are unambiguously outweighed by natural and human management-related factors. The NAPAP study came to the following conclusion:

'Available data suggest that natural stress factors (drought, insects, disease, temperature extremes), stand dynamics, and cultural /management practices are the major factors in observed changes of crop and forest condition...[F]or the agricultural systems studied, acidic precipitation has not been associated with crop growth or yield reduction at current ambient levels' (1990, pp. 18-168).

David Waugh's claims that acid rain increases 'the acidity of soil which, unless lime is added, reduces the quality of the crops' (1994b, p. 30) might seem plausible enough at first glance. However, crop harvesting produces soil acidity several times as fast as the highly acid rain of Central Europe (see Howells, 1995, p. 80). This is why agricultural soils must be routinely managed by ploughing (which can mobilise relatively basic podzols), liming, adding fertiliser (which precipitates acid-mobilised aluminium ions), and so on, to control pH and mineral levels (see Howells, 1995, p. 220, and NAPAP, 1990, pp. 18-70 to 18-71).

Textbook Evidence, Textbook Science

Despite scientific opinion on the subject, many school textbooks insist that acid rain inflicts acute damage on plant life. In part, these claims stem from a conflation of the acute pollutant doses characteristic of areas near industrial emissions sites and the more distant and dilute deposition of sulphur and nitrogen oxides in wet or dry form over large areas. For instance, the *Longman Revise Guide* to GCSE Chemistry mixes together these very different types of sulphur dioxide pollution: 'the gas [is carried] many hundreds of miles and it is now accepted that much pollution is carried to Scandinavian countries by the prevailing south-westerly winds common in Britain. The gas attacks plants, stonework and metal [and causes] damage to vegetation' (McElroy and Sadler, 1994, p. 242).[1] The impression given here is that large doses of sulphur dioxide gas from British factories

---

[1] The effects of acid rain on stonework so frequently commented upon are something of an exaggeration. NAPAP researchers found that 'field and laboratory experiments do not show a relationship between the amount of solids washed from the stone and the pH of the incident rainfall.' Using chemical analyses, the researchers compared the contributions of the different components of rainfall and dry precipitation to 'carbonate stone recession' in slabs placed at a 30° angle to the horizontal. They estimated that 'the wet deposition of hydrogen ion from all acid species in rain accounts for ~10 per cent of the chemical erosion of stone at the NAPAP field exposure sites.' Dry deposition of sulphur was found to contribute ~5 per cent to 20 per cent, while the dry deposition of nitric acid contributes ~2 per cent to 6 per cent, and the remainder was caused by the interaction between carbon monoxide in the air and calcite in the stone (NAPAP, 1990, pp. 19-162). Cities with serious air pollution levels can expect to experience accelerated stone erosion from the dry deposition of pollutants, but sulphuric and nitric acids in rain cannot be argued to have a big impact on the rate of disintegration of stonework.

are attacking Scandinavian vegetation. In fact, '[a]tmospheric deposition and concentrations of air contaminants [such as SO_2 gas] are typically only great enough to cause acute injury...to agricultural or forest vegetation in the immediate vicinity of point sources of air pollution' (NAPAP, 1990, pp. 18-30). This sort of highly localised pollution is very different from the long-distance transport of sulphur and nitrogen oxides and their subsequent ionisation and dissolution in rainfall that has caused so much worry in Scandinavia. By the beginning of the 1990s, local 'areas of eastern Europe and Asia' were the only places unlucky enough to be 'experienc[ing] regular incidence of [air pollutant] concentrations capable of causing acute injury to vegetation' (*ibid.*, pp. 18-63). The photograph of withered and blackened conifers in Poland displayed in David Waugh's *Key Geography* text was probably taken in one of these areas. However, Waugh misleadingly labels the photo: 'Acid rain damage to trees, Poland' (1994b, p. 31). By implication, acid rain causes the same devastation of trees across Scandinavia and the rest of Western Europe, although clearly that is not the case.

Some educators set out to confirm the harmful effects of acid rain on plants in classroom experiments, despite scientific opinion to the contrary. One Key Stage 3 science text recommends answering the question '[d]oes acid rain really damage plants?' with the help of an experiment 'to see how acid affects the growth of cress seeds' (Johnson *et al.*, 1995a, p. 5).[2] From the outset, the utility of comparing hydroponically cultivated cress seeds with crops or conifers growing in soils of different sorts is questionable. Furthermore, the 'Help Sheet' recommendations on how to set up the experiment contain no guidance as to the pH level that should be chosen to approximate real-world precipitation (Johnson *et al.*, 1995b, p. 53).[3] Pouring water that might be as sour as vinegar over cress seeds in a

---

[2] Similar experiments are described in the WWF's *'My World': A Resource Pack for Primary Teachers*, ed. Julie Smart (1992), pp. 9-11 of *Issue 1: Exploring the Earth*, and p. 14 of *Issue 2: Exploring the Air*.

[3] One wonders how the experiment turned out for those pupils and teachers in areas with acidic rain who decided to compare cress growth in pH-neutral water with growth in local rainwater rather than following textbook instructions to use concentrated sulphuric acid in preparing their test sample.

cotton swab cannot possibly shed much light on the effects of acid rain on plants growing in natural or agricultural soil conditions. The experiment provides little insight into the use of good science to test a causal hypothesis. While the goal of giving pupils a hands-on way of grappling with environmental problems in the classroom is laudable, textbook authors should make sure that they are not urging children to conduct purely rhetorical science.

Acid Rain: The Problem for Lakes and Streams

The impact of acid rain is most serious in the case of aquatic environments. It does demonstrably lead to soil acidification in sensitive areas (primarily those with poor, granitic soils), and thence to the acidification of lakes and streams in the vicinity. This can kill fish and other aquatic life (see Howells, 1995, pp. 220-21). Most textbook accounts pick up on this. For instance, Johnson *et al.* list the 'release of toxic metals like aluminium from the soil' and 'death of fish and fresh-water invertebrates' among the effects of acid rain (Johnson *et. al.,*1995b, p. 54), although they do not point out that the aluminium released is toxic to fish and not to humans.[4] The *Longman Revise Guide* in GCSE Chemistry notes that rain laced with sulphuric acid decreases 'the pH of water, and, when this arrives in rivers and streams, it causes fishes and plants to die' (McElroy and Sadler, 1994, p. 142).

---

[4] Barton states that the '[a]queous aluminium [washed into streams by acid rain] prevents the gills of fish from working, *as well as being poisonous to other organisms, including humans*' (1993, pp. 206-07, my emphasis). Aqueous aluminium is toxic to animals other than fish only at much higher doses than can be found in acidified streams. The NAPAP survey made the following conclusion about the increase in human exposure to all different kinds of metals due to acid rain: 'Incremental exposures to metals due to acid precipitation alone are not likely to be associated with any increased risk of human health effects except possibly for lead and mercury' (NAPAP, 1990, pp. 23-146). Basically, it seems that heavy metal exposure is or is not a problem in a given area for reasons largely independent of the degree of acidity in local waters. In the NAPAP study, increased mercury exposure was considered to be a possible problem only for persons eating a diet very rich in fish taken from highly acidified waters. This seems likely to be a rare scenario for obvious reasons. Dangerous lead exposure would be a problem only for populations already drinking water with lead concentrations near the borderline of acceptable levels (perhaps because of lead soldering in old pipes), and then only if their drinking water had been acidified by rain to 'extreme levels' (*ibid.*, pp. 23-147).

Usually the most severely acidified sites are small high-elevation lakes and streams. These sites are dominated by the geological and vegetational conditions of their limited catchment area which may be conducive to acidification. Furthermore, they get most of their water directly through rainfall, unlike larger lowland water bodies which are fed primarily through underground seepage channels containing buffering minerals (personal communication from Howells, 8 October 1996). This small-lake bias in high acidity lakes is evident in a table relating size to acidity levels in Swedish lakes (Table 1) presented as part of a sample exam question in the Biology *Longman Revise Guide* (Barker *et al.*, 1994, p. 293). In fact, this feature is the most immediately striking aspect of the data: of the 83,000-odd lakes tested, 4,628 have a pH level of 5.0 or lower, and 4,000 of these are in the smallest category, between 0.01-0.1 km^2 in area, while no lakes larger than 10 km^2 are this acidic.

Unfortunately, this important, indeed outstanding, feature of the data is studiously overlooked by the authors. The fact is never commented upon or explained in the course of the question, something of a lost opportunity to reveal more about the nature of the acid rain problem. Indeed, the table is used purely mechanically; pupils have only to read a number from it. In another section of the question, the authors mention the fact that 400 of the lakes observed were treated with slaked lime, and ask for a reason why smaller lakes were treated rather than larger lakes. This might seem like an opportunity for readers to comment on the relationship between size and acidity displayed so clearly in the table. However, the authors specifically caution students *not* to comment on the fact that smaller lakes are generally the worst affected: 'Smaller lakes are not necessarily more acidic than larger lakes [see Table 1], so it's best to avoid referring to this' (*ibid.*, p. 309). In effect, students are asked to suppress notice of one of the most striking features of the data. This is worrying, since the authors are themselves GCSE examiners, and probably closely reflect the approach of those who set the exams. I do not wish to suggest that the question should have led pupils to conclude that acid rain is an insignificant problem on the basis that predominantly small lakes are affected. However, as it stands the question makes a

31

TABLE 1:
pH Value of Various Lakes in Sweden

Size of Lakes in Km²	Number of Lakes			
	pH 5·0 or lower	pH 5·0-5·9	pH 6·0-6·9	pH 7·0 or higher
bigger than 100	0	0	9	13
10-100	0	2	260	100
1-10	28	380	3,000	590
0·1-1	600	4,400	12,700	1,550
00·1-0·1	4,000	24,500	28,500	2,700
Total	4,628	29,282	44,469	4,953

Source: Barker *et al., Biology Longman Revise Guide*, p. 293. Reprinted by
permission of Addison Wesley Longman Ltd.

FIGURE 2:
**Range of pH Values in which Populations of
Various Organisms Cannot Survive in Lakes**

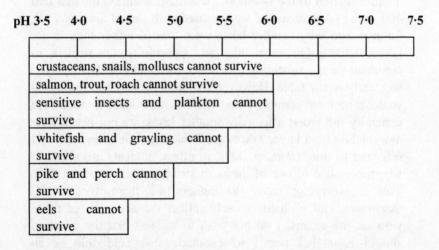

Source : Barker *et al., ibid.*, reprinted by permission of Addison Wesley
Longman Ltd., p.293.

singularly unimpressive use of the data. It does not encourage pupils to 'read' the data in the sense of looking for patterns in it and asking what leads to those patterns, something which is absolutely vital to the scientific use – indeed, to any thoughtful use – of quantitative data.

Another important part of the acidification story that is left out of textbooks is the contribution of land use practices to soil acidity. Gwyneth Howells writes that '[v]egetative growth, especially of trees and permanent grasslands, causes soil acidification by withdrawal of base cations into the above-ground biomass' (1995, p. 19). The intensive cultivation of conifer forests tends to remove these bases, accelerating the natural process of slow acidification that results from permanent afforestation. Sitka spruce, a fast-growing conifer favoured by foresters, 'creates good conditions for aluminium in the runoff water' and releases more than usual of the nitrates from polluted precipitation into nearby waters (personal communication from Howells, 8 October 1996). It is ironic that the very forests which are supposedly wilting under attack by poisonous rain are in fact able to grow so vigorously that they exacerbate the problem of acidification in surface waters. Any effort to deal with the latter must involve careful attention to the way in which land near water bodies is used.

Culprits and Remedies

School textbooks almost uniformly focus on reductions in sulphur emissions as the way to control the consequences of acidification. Often, they emphasise Britain's role as an 'exporter' of sulphur dioxide. One Geography book for 10 to 11-year-olds features a bar chart showing sulphur dioxide emission and deposition in European countries. Britain has the highest SO_2 emissions of the countries shown apart from West and East Germany taken together, and the text comments that 'you can see that some countries, such as Britain, emit more sulphur dioxide than is deposited by them' (Marsden and Marsden, 1995, p. 30).[5] Another map on the same page makes a clear connection

---

[5] Readers looking at the map closely might wonder why Italy and France are apparently not suffering from acid rain despite the fact that their sulphate deposition figures are both substantially higher than Sweden's.

between UK emissions and acid rain in Scandinavia. McElroy and Sadler in the Chemistry *Longman Revise Guide* comment that 'it is now accepted that much pollution is carried to Scandinavian countries by the prevailing south-westerly winds common in Britain'(1994, p. 242). In his unit on acid rain, David Waugh cites figures for emissions reductions planned in the UK: 'Britain is committed to reducing sulphur dioxide emissions by 60 per cent of their 1980 levels by the year 2000 and by 71 per cent by the year 2005. So far they have been reduced by 30 per cent. Some European countries say this is too little and is taking too long' (Waugh, 1994b, p. 31). In fact, the emphasis on reducing emissions in Britain to solve acid rain problems in Scandinavia is misplaced.

Recent computer modelling estimates indicate that Britain's sulphur contributions 'could be only about 8% of the total deposited in Norway and about 3% in Sweden' (Howells, 1995, p. 19). Clearly, even cutting smokestack emissions in Britain to zero would do little to improve the situation in Scandinavia. Emissions controls in Britain must be justified on a local basis.

The evidence on surface water acidification throughout Britain is hard to assess, since there has been no extensive and methodologically rigorous national survey like the one conducted in the US under the National Acidic Precipitation Assessment Program (NAPAP). Howells summed up the current evidence for the UK in 1995: 'Areas in Britain considered susceptible to acidification are predominantly ... in western and upland areas.' Data from water authorities over the course of a decade on English and Welsh rivers 'provided little evidence of acidified waters or trends of increased acidity,' and 18 Scottish sites showed 'a fall in pH from 6.6 to 6.3 between the late 1960s and 1983-85, but this change was unrelated to changes in sulphate.' Of the upland tarns and streams most likely to be affected, those that showed signs of acidification tended to be 'in areas of high rainfall and base-poor bedrock and thin soils rather than in areas of low rain pH or high sulphate concentration, although they have high deposition; chloride is the main anion present' (Howells, 1995, p. 119). These sensitive upland waters, like the Scottish rivers investigated, lacked the saturation with sulphate ions that is the signature of acid rain damage in Scandinavia and the US. More recent follow-up studies that also look for evidence of nitrogen oxides pollution in UK waters have also tended to come up with 'little significant to report' (personal communication from Howells, 8 October 1996).

By contrast, there is more evidence that afforestation in Britain might be contributing to surface-water acidification. The interim report to the Department of the Environment on acidification in UK fresh waters noted that

'[p]roductive forest now accounts for 6.3% of the total land area of Great Britain, almost a threefold increase since the formation of the Forestry Commission in 1919. Much of the afforested area is concentrated in uplands. In mid-Wales, for example ... coniferous forest now accounts for 21.5% of the land area. This represents a seven-fold increase since 1948. By contrast, broadleaved woodland accounts for only 1.7%' (Warren *et al.*, 1986, p. 34, cited in Howells, 1995).

It makes economic sense to use fast-growing conifers in poor-soiled upland areas for forestry plantations, but this is also a recipe for acidification of surrounding waters. Warren and his colleagues reported that 'the fishery status of surface waters in Scotland and Wales is generally poorer in catchments subject to afforestation' (*ibid.*, p. 37). Pine trees make less striking environmental villains than power station smokestacks, but sometimes they can be more effective in killing fish.

Where silvicultural practices contribute significantly to surface water acidification, foresters will have to lime catchment areas if they want to save nearby streams and lakes from decline. Liming is also an important part of any response to acidification from sulphur or nitrogen deposition. Build-up of strongly acidic anions in the soil and lakes means that it may take up to a century, even if current emissions were reduced by more than 80 per cent, for lakes to return to normal pH levels. Given this fact, catchment liming which, in contrast to treating lakes directly, elevates pH and increases the availability of minerals like calcium which are important to fish respiration in a controlled, ecologically undisruptive way for substantial periods (Howells, 1995, p. 6) is crucial if aquatic communities in pollution-damaged areas are to be restored in the short term. Thus, the common textbook assertion that liming is too expensive (Barton, 1993, p. 207) and

35

inadequate, 'like taking aspirin to cure cancer' (Johnson *et al.*, 1995, p. 5), misses the point that any strategy to mitigate the effects of acid rain should include the technique.

The acidification of fresh-water and sylvian environments demands a variety of different responses. Given the long-term effects of acid rain on forests and the more dramatic damage it does to fresh-water life, well-targeted efforts to reduce anthropogenic sulphur and nitrogen emissions can only be of benefit to the environment. At the same time, land-use practices must be recognised as a factor that can have an equal and sometimes greater impact on acid levels in soils and nearby waters. Additionally, a programme of repeated catchment liming is a crucial component of any acidity-recovery programme for damaged aquatic environments.

The history of efforts to reduce sulphur emission rates shows that legislated ceilings on pollution levels that industry as a whole must meet in whatever way it sees fit are generally superior to state-imposed technological fixes, such as mandatory scrubber implementation laws. Technological requirements discourage other potentially cheaper ways of limiting emissions, such as using cleaner coal or pre-cleaning the fuel used for power generation (Ackerman and Hassler, 1981).

Sulphur deposition rates have been declining since before 1980 in Europe (and since about 1970 in the US), and nitrogen compounds, primarily from vehicle emissions, are likely to take over the leading role as acidifying agents. Nitrogen emissions, largely from motor vehicles, are likely to be more difficult to control than the point sources that generate the bulk of sulphur pollution (Howells, 1995, pp. 215-16). On the other hand, of course, reducing motor vehicle emissions has the added benefit of improving the air quality in cities.

In any case, textbooks generally do not tell the story of acid rain very well. They tend to mix up different kinds of air pollution, over-dramatise the effects of acid rain on plants, omit the important role of land-use practices in environmental acidification, and perpetuate the myth of Britain as a primary culprit in Scandinavia's acid rain problem. Environmental education needs to shed the version of the acid rain issue which it has inherited from the 1980s and re-tell the story in a way that does better justice to the current state of knowledge and to the choices involved in making good environmental policy.

An Alternative Textbook Passage

In the past several decades, environmentalists have been worried about acid rain pollution. The acids they are referring to come mostly from coal-fired power plants, which emit sulphur dioxide (SO_2), and fossil-fuel-burning engines like those in cars, which emit nitrogen oxides (NO, NO_2). These chemicals are carried into the air and then either fall to the Earth in dry form anywhere up to about two hundred miles from their source, or are converted into sulphuric and nitric acid high in the atmosphere and eventually fall to earth, sometimes much farther away, as acid in rain.

When West European forests underwent a decline in the 1980s, there were fears that acid rain was damaging forests and crops. Scientists now think that acid rain is unlikely to be the primary cause of the 'die-back' in European forests that took place in the 1980s. Only plants which are near dirty industrial polluters have been shown to suffer immediate damage from acid pollution, and this is rare in Western Europe.

The effect of acid rain on crops is insignificant, and the agricultural cycle of growing and harvesting crops acidifies the land much more quickly than acid rain can. This is one of the reasons that farmers must use fertilisers to keep their fields productive year after year. At the same time, it does seem that acid rain causes long-term changes in the nutrient cycles of forests that can cause a slow-down in plant growth.

Acid rain also causes the gradual acidification of soil in areas with bedrock lacking in bases (chemicals which neutralise the effects of acids). Once soil is acidified, the water that runs through it and into streams and lakes becomes acidic, and this kills fish and other aquatic life. Often the most badly acidified water bodies are small lakes and streams in mountainous areas. Once the soil in an area has become acidified, it will remain so for many years (50-100 years perhaps) unless lime is spread on the catchment area (the soil near the water) every few years.

Acid rain is not the only problem for vulnerable upland soils and waters. The fast-growing conifers that are used in modern

37

forestry tend to leach bases out of the soil as they grow. When they are cut down and taken away, acid soil is left behind, and the aquatic life in nearby waters suffers.

Worries about the effects of acid rain have led to legislation limiting sulphur emissions in Europe and America. The Scandinavian countries have led the call for this sort of legislation, since their surface waters are some of the worst affected by acidification, most of it caused by acid rain from nearby countries. It is often claimed that Britain's pollution is at fault for the acid rain problem in Scandinavia. However, recent computer models suggest that Britain's emissions could be responsible for no more than 8 per cent of the total sulphur deposited in Norway and 3 per cent of the total in Sweden. Power plants and cars in Central Europe are more at fault for acid rain damage to Scandinavian waters.

Reducing sulphur and nitrogen emissions in Britain may help British forests and fresh water environments in the long run, although it will not do much to solve the acid rain problem in Scandinavia. If the effects of acidification are to be remedied, emissions from industries and automobiles must be reduced, and fragile soils used for forestry and the soil near acidified water bodies must be limed periodically to prevent or reverse acidification.

3. Global Warming

The hypothesis of human-induced global warming rests on a fairly simple principle. Carbon dioxide and a handful of other gases which keep the Earth at a generally stable, warm temperature are being augmented by human activity, and will lead to a warming of the planet. The conjecture is scientifically plausible, and worth investigating. Beyond this point, scientists disagree widely on just about every point of the global warming story, partly because the mechanisms which control the planet's climate are imperfectly understood and partly because so much of the debate concerns hypothetical changes and assertions that cannot be falsified until more time has passed. However, enough is known about climatic mechanisms and about the temperature record to date to permit some judgements about which versions of the greenhouse story are likely to be more or less plausible.

The Greenhouse Effect in School Texts

Textbooks give somewhat differing accounts of global warming. One of the more detailed discussions, in David Waugh's *Key Geography for GCSE*, begins with the observation that

> '[t]he natural greenhouse effect is essential as without it the Earth's average temperature would be 33°C lower than it is. Recent human activity has led to an increase in greenhouse gases. This is causing world temperatures to rise, a process known as global warming' (Waugh, 1994b, p. 28).

Other texts are more cautious about the assertion that human-induced warming is actually occurring. One group of GCSE Biology authors notes that '[t]here is still some uncertainty about whether recent increases in the world's temperature are due to global warming, or part of a regular series of long-term temperature fluctuations which have occurred in the past' (Barker *et al.*, 1994, p. 306). This latter point is quite true. A period of relative cooling in the Northern Hemisphere that began 500 years ago called the 'Little Ice Age' ended about 100 years ago. This cooling period was not associated with a fall in CO_2

gases in the atmosphere, but the warming that ended it occurred contemporaneously with man-made CO_2 emissions. Given this history, comments the climatologist Robert Balling Jr., 'it remains largely unknown whether any warming this century is predominantly from emissions of greenhouse gases or from some processes that brought us rather naturally out of the Little Ice Age' (Balling, 1992, p. 50).

Whatever their difference of opinion about the reasons for current climatic trends, almost all textbooks that discuss global warming agree that the burning of fossil fuels and deforestation constitute the major potential sources of a human-induced 'greenhouse effect'. On the latter point, Barker, Jones and Millican comment that '[d]eforestation accounts for about 20 per cent of the increased CO_2 levels in the atmosphere ... [T]imber removal means there are less trees to absorb CO_2 by photosynthesis' (1994, p. 306). In fact, while it is true that burning or rotting trees put CO_2 into the atmosphere, the idea that mature forests like the Amazon rainforest are the 'lungs of the planet', absorbing huge quantities of CO_2, is unfounded. These 'climax' forests operate on closed nutrient cycles, and 'have been recycling the same amount of carbon for centuries' (de Miranda, 1994, p. 155). If one pauses to consider the situation, this becomes obvious; plants can only absorb net amounts of carbon if they are increasing in biomass. Ancient forests like that of the Amazon are about as tall and as dense as they are going to get. The only forests that absorb net amounts of carbon dioxide are young, growing ones, usually those that have been recently cut by humans or damaged by fire or storms. Deforestation can cause a one-off rise in atmospheric CO_2, and represents a loss of wildlife habitat, but it does not diminish 'the rate at which carbon dioxide is removed from the atmosphere during photosynthesis' (Barton, 1993, p. 101).

Forecasts...

Nevertheless, it is true that CO_2 levels are on the increase as a result of human activities, especially the burning of fossil fuels (see Balling, 1992, p. 22). Textbook authors are quick to claim that the rise in CO_2 levels will lead to a sudden warming trend. The authors of the *Longman Revise Guide* in GCSE Biology state that '[p]ossible temperature increases during the next 50 years have been suggested in the range of 1.5°C to 5.5°C, if concentrations of green house gases rise at current rates' (Barker *et al.*, 1994, p. 306). David Waugh cites '[e]stimates [which] suggest that, without controls on greenhouse gas emissions, temperatures could rise by up to 0.5° C each decade over the next 100 years (graph D)' (1994b, p. 28). This figure is twice as slow as Barker's upper estimate, but it still implies a 10-fold jump in the rate of warming in the near future. Despite being couched in hypothetical language – there are 'suggestions' that 'temperatures could rise' – these predictions have a ring of authority to them. They almost seem like fact when stripped of the scientific uncertainty about the role of oceans, clouds, and geological weathering processes that qualifies them in the academic arena. Educational texts tend to lend extra rhetorical weight to predictions of climate change, both by muting the uncertainties of the global warming thesis, and in the very presentation of the forecasts themselves.

David Waugh's graphical presentation of potential climate change over the next 40 years (see Figure 3), is strongly rhetorical. The graph, which also appears in the Philip's *Environmental Atlas for Children* (Wright, 1993, p. 21), contrasts what will happen to the global temperature by 2020 if 'present trends continue' with the situation if 'drastic cuts in emissions in the 1990s' are undertaken. In the first case, the temperature rises to +1.5°C above 1960s temperatures, while the other line shows a stabilisation at perhaps a tenth of a degree above the 1990 temperature (Waugh, 1994b, p. 29). Surprisingly, the graph shows the temperatures of both post-1990 trends oscillating quite as much as the recorded, pre-1990 figures. This is presumably done for aesthetic effect, since if taken at face value it implies a staggering degree of precision in forecasting. The symmetry of past and future in the graph is a rhetorical device that helps downplay the uncertainty of the estimates it represents.[1]

---

[1] Already, subsequent temperature readings have fallen below even the 'drastic emissions cuts' line (*cf.* Michaels and Knappenberger, 1996, p. 167).

FIGURE 3:
The Rise in Average Temperatures Caused by Greenhouse Gases, 1960-2020

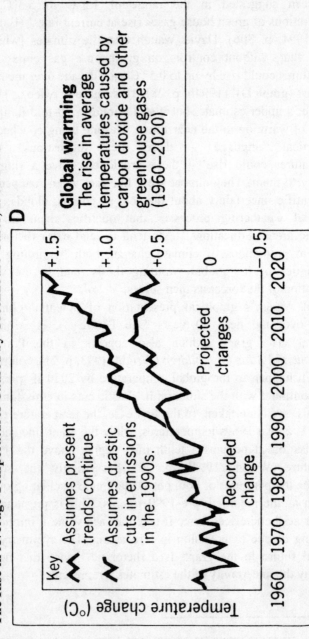

Source: Reproduced with permission from p. 29 of *Key Geography for GCSE: Book 2*, by David Waugh (1994b) © Stanley Thornes (Publishers) Ltd.

The basic figures behind Waugh and Wright's graph did not come out of thin air, however. The Policymakers' Summary of the first Intergovernmental Panel on Climate Change report in 1990 predicted 'a warming of 1.5°C between 1990 and 2025' (Michaels and Knappenberger, 1996, p. 163). What the IPCC and the textbook authors who cite them do not mention is that the computer models used to generate these sorts of forecasts substantially over-predict present temperatures. Given the increases in atmospheric CO_2 to date, an estimated 40 per cent rise over the past 100 years, 'climate models typically predict a warming of at least 1.0°C' (Balling, 1992, pp. 79-80), over twice the observed warming of less than 0.5°C (see also Emsley, 1996, p. 167). Failing to predict the future accurately is the common lot of human beings, scientists included. But a failure to predict the present is embarrassing.

The IPCC has subsequently tried to address this problem by resorting to the hypothesis that industrial emissions of SO_2 gas, the same chemical responsible for acid rain, has exerted a cooling effect on temperatures in the Northern Hemisphere. Adding a cooling element like sulphate to computer models of the 'greenhouse effect' does, unsurprisingly, give a better fit to the temperature changes observed; it helps to bring down the overshoot of the global warming models. However, the sulphate cooling hypothesis fails on a number of tests, and it seems that it cannot explain away the errors of the climatological models (Balling, 1995, pp. 108-09, Michaels and Knappenberger, 1996, pp. 171-76).

Thus, the failure of computer models to 'predict' the present, their inadequacy in the face of the only empirical test that can be put to them, is a major part of the global warming story, and one that should feature in textbook accounts. Some other aspects of the climatic record over the last century accord better with the computer models. There seem to have been some increases in cloud coverage and precipitation over the last century (Balling, 1992, pp. 78-79), and over much of the globe, observed warming has taken place predominantly at night and during the colder months of the year (*ibid.*, p. 52, p. 92). While this pattern of temperature smoothing cannot be taken as proof positive of a human impact on the climate, it does indicate that if we are in the midst of global warming, it is of a much more moderate sort than that portrayed in the most dramatic accounts.

Editing Texts on the Effects of CO₂

The evidence for modest (if any) anthropogenic climate change calls into question the predictions of catastrophe contained in many educational texts. For instance, the authors of the *Longman Review Guide* in GCSE Biology comment that '[i]n tropical areas of the world, decreased availability of water might lead to the formation of deserts. In coastal areas throughout the world, some melting of polar ice-caps would result in flooding. Other predicted effects include the spread of tropical disease over a wider area, increased frequency of droughts, hurricanes and cyclones, and also forest fires' (Barker *et al.*, 1994, p. 306). While these events sound alarming, they all depend on warming trends that are much more extreme than those suggested by the patterns observed to date. As Michaels and Knappenberger comment:

'[v]irtually all of the apocalyptic scenarios that accompany the extremist vision of global warming – massive sea level rise caused by the melting of large areas of high-latitude ice, burning forests, starvation from global crop failures, and general ecological collapse – are fuelled by a dramatic warming of the summer days. It is, in fact, impossible to melt the polar ice during any other season; warming polar winter temperature merely results in a wetter atmosphere which produces more snow and enhances the icepack' (Michaels and Knappenberger, 1996, p. 161).

Just as ice packs might grow under the influence of moderate winter warming at the poles, so too just about every one of the disastrous circumstances mentioned by the *Longman* Biology authors could be predicted in reverse. Hurricanes may decrease if, as computer climate models predict, warming occurs disproportionately in higher latitudes, smoothing the Polar-Tropic temperature gradient that helps drive tropical storm systems (Balling, 1992, p. 113). Droughts may become rarer if the CO_2 blanket increases cloudiness and precipitation, as the climate models suggest, *and* if warming remains moderate and predominantly a night-time and cold-season phenomenon (*ibid.*, p. 109).

Instead of leading to the spread of existing deserts (see Wright, 1993, p. 20), the anthropogenic increase in CO_2 may assist the spread of plants on earth. Higher proportions of CO_2 in the air improve the efficiency with which plant leaves use water, since their leaf openings, which are constricted to prevent water loss, can photosynthesize more efficiently with a higher dose of carbon dioxide. This should increase their resistance to high temperatures and allow them to expand into more arid regions where water tends to be the limiting factor in plant growth. Likewise, CO_2-fertilised plants growing in nutrient-poor soils apparently put more energy into growing roots to probe deeper and more extensively for minerals, and higher concentrations of the gas may stimulate the activity of nitrogen-fixing bacteria (Idso, 1996, pp. 28-31).[2]

Textbook authors tend to be shy about giving credence to the potentially positive effects of higher levels of CO_2: Barker and his co-authors mention the idea that 'higher CO_2 concentrations' might lead to 'increased crop yields' but quickly add that 'insect pest populations might also increase and there might be less soil water available' (1994, p. 306). They are right that the fertilisation of plants by CO_2 would come as no great consolation if the worst fears of global warming, dramatically increasing daytime temperatures and a consequent increase in evaporation rates, were to come to pass. However, they miss the fact that higher levels of CO_2 reduce the rate of water loss in plants. And their mention of increases in pest populations seems a little unfair; of course increases in primary production rates would give insects more to feed on, but then the animals that prey on the insects would presumably benefit as well, and so on up the food chain. In biology textbook terms, if the base of the biomass pyramid widens, so will all the subsequent tiers.

---

[2] Idso's claim that higher CO_2 concentrations lead to increases in plant growth rate should be taken with a grain of salt, however. While this sort of effect does occur in the short run, over the longer term, the plants' growth slows as part of an inner feedback mechanism (personal communication from Elizabeth Newell, 2 June 1997).

There is a tradition in the popular literature of emphasising the negative and downplaying the positive effects that might follow from the human-induced 'greenhouse effect' (Bate, 1996, pp. 13-14n). Most schoolbooks display this same tendency. The standard justification for the bias towards pessimism is that 'by the time there is indisputable evidence for a link between greenhouse gas concentrations and global warming [and, presumably, the catastrophic consequences attendant upon it], the ecological problem will be too big to solve' (Barker *et al.*, 1994, p. 306). The mere possibility of these disaster scenarios necessitates action. As the presenter in a Shell educational video called 'Climate of Concern' states, 'to wait for final proof would be irresponsible' (Shell Film and Video Unit, 1991).

Policy

One of the problems with this clarion call to action on the basis of precaution, as noble as it sounds, is that making any dent in the amount of global warming predicted by the computer models is extremely difficult. Robert Balling Jr. quotes a graph from the 1990 IPCC report contrasting the progress of warming given 'business as usual' with that consequent on an impressive policy programme of moving to lower carbon-based fuels, achieving large efficiency increases, reversing deforestation, and so on. The action-oriented approach (assuming that it is feasible) manages to avert only a single degree Celsius of the projected 4° increase by the year 2100. Thinking back to the Waugh/Wright graph which shows the possibility of nearly stopping global warming over the course of 30 years, one can imagine quite how far the 'big cuts' in emissions would need to go – probably not far short of dismantling the present industrial economy.

Many scientists seem to agree with a more 'wait-and-see' approach to the issue. A letter dated February 1992 and signed by 'over fifty scientists, most of whom hold or once held leadership positions in the American Meteorological Society', expressed concern over the 'Earth Summit' to be held in Rio de Janeiro that summer. The letter warned that 'policy initiatives' over global warming 'derive from highly uncertain scientific theories. They are based on the unsupported assumption that catastrophic warming follows from the burning of fossil fuel and requires immediate action. We do not agree' (East *et al.*, 1994, p. 55). This represents the views of a large number of prominent scientists who are professionally knowledgeable about the issues involved in the global warming debate. The reputation of their discipline will be on the line if the 'greenhouse' scare turns out to have been a needless and possibly costly exercise in alarmism.[3]

Policy-makers are probably well advised to forgo any drastic action on the basis of fears over global warming, instead of waiting to assess climatic developments over the next few decades. Obviously, if warming suddenly jumped to the rate of 0.5°C a decade, the rate cited by Waugh and Wright, it might be prudent to begin taxing carbon emissions heavily. But until then, or until a slower but still serious pattern of warming becomes clearer, policy measures should probably be confined to those that make sense for other reasons – like abolishing existing energy subsidies and continuing to cut back on the production of CFCs, which pose a risk to the ozone layer and presently contribute almost a quarter to the estimated 'increased greenhouse effect' generated by humans (see Balling, 1992, p. 30).

Of course, the public should not forget entirely about the possibility of global warming. Fossil fuels reserves will probably last for another several centuries despite widespread belief to the contrary (see Chapter 2), and carbon dioxide levels may reach several times pre-industrial levels in the atmosphere before they are exhausted. The developed world must be ready to aid poorer countries if sea levels gradually rise enough to cause a problem. But the 'greenhouse effect' should not be taken as an excuse for calls to exaggerated and drastic action which would likely be very harmful if heeded.

Textbook authors who wish to deliver a more balanced account of global warming should put greater emphasis on the uncertainties associated with the theory. If they wish to cite the predictions of computerised climate models, they should

---

[3] The February letter can be contrasted with the petition circulated by the Union of Concerned Scientists in 1989 urging recognition of global warming as a threat to mankind. After several rounds of solicitations, the petition was eventually signed by some 700 scientists and subsequently published in *The New York Times*, but only three or four of the signatories had any involvement in climatology (Lindzen, 1994, p. 128).

investigate and clarify for their readers the extent to which those models manage or fail to predict current weather conditions. Authors who still feel compelled to recommend political action in the interests of slowing CO_2 emissions should be honest and specific with their readers about the benefits in terms of slowed CO_2 production and the economic costs that would likely be involved. It is hard to produce a balanced account of an issue that is the subject about which there is so much conjecture and so little hard evidence. However, educators must do their best to counteract the sensationalism that surrounds the subject and deliver an account that neither avoids nor exaggerates the scientific and political issues involved.

An Alternative Textbook Passage

The atmosphere contains a series of gases, including water vapour, carbon dioxide, methane, chlorofluorocarbons, and some others, which help to warm the Earth in what is called the 'greenhouse effect'. For the last century or so, industrial societies have been burning fossil fuels, releasing carbon dioxide into the atmosphere. The burning of forests has also increased the *level* of carbon dioxide in the air. However, reducing the number of trees in this way does not generally decrease the *rate* at which CO_2 is converted to oxygen. The reason is that most mature forests – like the rainforests of the Amazon – give off as much CO_2 as they take in. Only new-growth forests take in more carbon dioxide than they give off.

The level of carbon dioxide in the air has risen by about 40 per cent since the beginning of the industrial revolution (c. 1850). The worry about this rise in the CO_2 content of the atmosphere is that it might warm up the Earth by enhancing the natural 'greenhouse effect'. However, there is uncertainty about whether and how this will occur, and whether it will produce a strong enough effect to outweigh natural fluctuations in the climate. Some scientists have used computers to try to predict how fast global warming will occur based on a simplified model of the world's climate. These models have come up with all sorts of different predictions, depending on the assumptions that are used to generate them. One of the problems with these computer models is that they generally say the weather now should be warmer than it actually is, given the 40 per cent rise in CO_2 levels since industrial emissions began. The models do not do very well because scientists have yet to figure out just how clouds, the oceans, and geological wearing contribute to the global climate.

The effects of any possible global warming depend a lot on where and when the warming occurs. Dramatic warming during the day in the summer would spread drought, while night-time or winter warming might be helpful. If warming is concentrated at the poles during the summer, it might lead to a melting of the polar ice caps and a rise in sea levels, which would be a disaster for coastal communities. On the other hand, if it happens mostly in winter at the poles, the ice caps would not melt, and might actually grow because of wetter, snowier Arctic winters. If the build-up of CO_2 causes increased cloudiness over the Earth, as most computer models of the climate suggest, and is moderate in scope, the warming that occurs would be mostly in winter and at night, and so would have a generally mild set of effects. If drastic warming occurs, it will probably bring all of the nastier effects like drought and rises in sea level with it. More CO_2 in the atmosphere will be good news for plants in dry areas, since in a high-CO_2 atmosphere, crops and other plants will use water, and possibly soil nutrients, more efficiently.

Some people have urged immediate action to curb CO_2 emissions on the grounds that even the possibility of global warming calls for action now. The problem is that it takes very big cuts in fossil fuel use to make a significant dent in warming forecasts. Because we rely on fossil fuels so much in our everyday life – to get us from place to place, to keep us warm, to generate the electricity that we rely on in so many different ways – cutting back drastically on their use is likely to be very costly indeed.

There are some simple strategies to reduce the human impact on the climate that look less difficult. Chlorofluorocarbons, or CFCs, have been shown to have destructive effects on the Earth's ozone layer, and are such powerful greenhouse gases that, by some estimates, they account for about a quarter of the total warming effect created by human activity. Continuing international reductions of CFC production makes sense. So does energy conservation where it saves money.

49

Of course, the developed countries have a responsibility to come to the aid of poorer countries if serious effects like a substantial rise in sea level begin to materialise; after all, the rich economies of the world are the ones burning most of the world's fossil fuels. But until we have a better understanding of what the human 'greenhouse effect' will look like, it is probably best to wait and see.

4. Desertification

The Africa of Geography schoolbooks is in a perpetual state of ecological crisis. Its fragile plains are being stretched to breaking point by runaway population growth, its soils are washing away, and deserts are spreading over the surface of the continent. Only vigorous countermeasures, presumably conducted by governments of the region in conjunction with experts in the developed world, can roll back the despoliation of Africa by its unwitting inhabitants.

The Desert's Spread

Many Geography textbooks tell basically the same story about the unsustainable farming and herding practices that are putting Africa's grasslands at risk. As the authors of the *Blackwell Geography Project* state:

> '[a]round 700 million people live in desert regions' [defined in the text as areas with less than 250mm of rainfall a year]. 'Most live in rural areas and support themselves by keeping livestock like cattle, goats and sheep. These animals can *overgraze* the land (eat away all the natural vegetation). In times of drought, overgrazing is a very serious problem. Natural vegetation protects the soil. The roots of trees and plants bind the soil together. When no trees, shrubs, bushes or grass are left, the soil is *eroded* by sudden, heavy rainfall, or by winds blowing it away. Overgrazing leads to erosion; the next stage can be desert' (Punnett *et al.*, 1989, p. 38).

The text goes on to spell out other ways in which misuse of the land leads to desertification. These include 'cutting down trees for firewood, clearing land for growing crops, using poorly-designed irrigation, and overcultivation (often in an attempt to provide food for a growing population)' (*ibid.*, p. 38).

In some textbooks, these causes are arranged in a downward 'desertification spiral' (see Figure 4), which helps emphasise the relentless irreversibility of the process by which 'overgrazing, overcultivation, deforestation, drought, fire, [and] soil erosion' lead to 'desert...sustained by the hot, dry climate' (Kemp *et al.*,

1992, p. 37. As the author of the *Longman Revise Guide* for GCSE Science emphasises, the downward spiral into desertification, once complete, 'is almost impossible to reverse' (Barton, 1993, p. 101).

In the 1991 GCSE exam set by the London East Anglian Group, the desertification narrative is framed in a neat flow chart showing the way in which the primary factors of population growth and climatic change lead step-by-step through over-exploitation of the land and drought to desertification (London East Anglian Group, Paper 2, Thursday 6 June 1991 – Afternoon, Geography [Syllabus B], p. 22). Desertification maps usually show areas of desertification (or the 'risk of desertification') throughout the world: in the American West, on the South American pampas, in Australia and the Middle East as well as in Africa (see Wright, 1993, p. 14; Foskett *et al.*, 1987, p. 76; Waugh, 1994b, p. 48), as if to emphasise the 'global' nature of the problem.[1] However, the basic model of population growth, overcultivation and overgrazing, gives away the fact that the desertification story is really set in the Third World, and above all in Africa.

The idea that the Sahara is marching southward is not new. Colonial administrators in the 1930s worried about the report by E.P. Stebbing, a forester from the Indian Forest Service who wrote prolifically about desertification on the basis of a trip through West Africa (Swift, 1996, p. 74). Stebbing's identification of the main causes of the problem find an echo in today's school textbooks. They include: 'indigenous forms of

---

[1] There are some efforts to justify the extension of the desertification danger to developed countries. For instance, there is a box entitled 'Desertification in the USA' on the next page of the exam. The text describes how some of the 'semi-desert areas of Western USA' that are under irrigation to make them agriculturally productive have come under stress from salinification of the upper layers of the soil. 'Gradually the desert is extending once again' (London East Anglian Group, Paper 2, Thursday 6 June 1991 – Afternoon, Geography [Syllabus B], p. 23). It is hard to see how the problems with irrigated farming in the Southwest of the United States, which is linked to below-cost water provision to farmers in the region (Anderson and Leal, 1991, p. 102), forms part of a larger, global desertification crisis linked to overpopulation and climate change.

FIGURE 4:
The Desertification Spiral

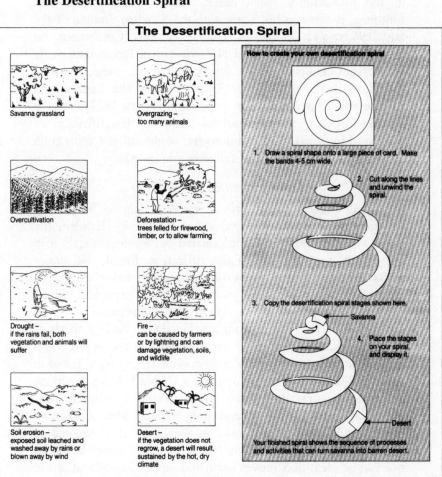

Source: Kemp *et al., Access to Geography Book 3: Key Stage 3*, 1992, p. 37, reprinted by permission of Oxford University Press.

land use, made more damaging by population growth resulting from the ending of local warfare and improvements in health, resulting in a reduced area available for cultivation, and a large increase in animal numbers' (*ibid.*, p. 75). After some wet years in the mid-century when desertification was more or less forgotten, it came to life again with the Sahelian drought of the late 1960s and 1970s. A United Nations Conference on Desertification and later the UN Environment Programme made extravagant claims about the progress of the problem, claiming that desertification 'threatens 35 per cent of the Earth's land surface and 20 per cent of its population...[since 1977] the land irretrievably lost through various forms of desertification or destroyed to desert-like conditions has continued at 6 million ha annually as reported in 1977' (cited in *ibid.*, p. 81).

The Desertification Mirage

Subsequent research has proved these claims to be grossly exaggerated. The Lund University study led by Helldén, the 'most comprehensive research' carried out on desertification in the Sudan, a classic site of desertification, found: 'No major shifts in the northern cultivation limit...No major change in vegetation cover and crop productivity was identified, which could not be explained by varying rainfall characteristics' (Swift, 1996, p. 84). The Swedish team concluded that 'the hypothesis of a secular, man-made trend towards desert-like conditions could not be confirmed in other dryland areas of Africa either' (cited in *ibid.*, p. 84). Another study, done by a United Nations expert on desertification in 1988, also came to the conclusion that, '[a]ttractive though the "encroaching Sahara" idea is, it is no more credible now than it was in Stebbing's day' (quoted in Morris, 1995, pp. 38-39). The 'border' of the Sahara, so far as one can be identified, moves north and south with fluctuations in rainfall levels. The Sahelian vegetation, being adapted to take rapid advantage of any increases in rainfall, tends to reclaim temporarily 'desertified' lands quickly at the end of a drought. Despite their frequent characterisation as a 'fragile environment' (see Waugh, 1994b, pp. 48-49), semi-arid grasslands are actually quite robust; they need to be to withstand the fluctuations in climate that are inherent to their location. The sometimes decade-long droughts common to the Sahel may have a devastating impact on the area's inhabitants, but they are cyclical in nature and, by all available evidence, do not lead to the permanent advance of the desert.

Desertification in the Curriculum

So why does the desertification story persist in school textbooks? One simple reason is that learning about the issue is explicitly required in the National Curriculum's Attainment Targets. At the final pre-GCSE attainment level in physical geography, pupils are expected to be able to 'explain how desertification in semi-arid lands may result from physical processes and human activities' (DES, 1991a, p. 17). Desertification also shows up in the science curriculum as a way of illustrating 'the basic scientific principles associated with a major change in the biosphere' (DES, 1991b, p. 26).

The need to teach about a problem which does not exist puts some stresses on educators. As long as they stick to flow diagrams with their seemingly implacable, step-by-step logic of decline, the texts have an air of grim plausibility to them. But the abysmal quality of the evidence behind the desertification story begins to show when it is mapped on the actual landscape. For instance, a question on the 1991 GCSE exam in Geography features a map 'showing areas of the world experiencing more frequent droughts leading to desertification' (London East Anglian Group, 3 June 1991, Geography (Syllabus A), Paper 2, p. 5). This particular map shows areas of 'desert (rainfall less than 200 mm per year)' and areas of 'desertification (rainfall 200-400 mm per year)'. In an exercise that does nothing to teach an inquiring and intelligent use of geographical data, pupils are told to fill in isohyets for 200 mm and 400 mm of rainfall on a map of West Africa, then label the area in-between 'desertification' and that north of it 'desert' (3 June 1991, Paper 2, p. 6). Desertification is hard to define, but linking simple rainfall levels[2] with the whole package of poor land-use practices that is supposed to lead to desert advance is ridiculous and

---

[2] A proper index of aridity includes information about the rate of evapotranspiration as well as rainfall.

arbitrary. Among other things, this approach implies that most of the Western United States is on its way to becoming a desert. The desertification map also labels central Argentina a 'desert,' although pupils who took the next exam in the same series would have come across a map of South America showing the same area to be 'land of medium suitability for farming' (6 June 1991, Paper 2, p. 8)! These kinds of inconsistencies make one wonder how seriously the exam's authors take their own maps and diagrams.

David Waugh's discussion of desertification in his *Key Geography for GCSE* (1994b) illustrates the difficulties faced by authors who try to teach the desertification story in the face of the evidence against it. Waugh is aware that the desertification scare of the 1970s and 1980s turned out to be just that, and he goes about making a revealing set of qualifications to his version of the desertification narrative. To his credit, he notes that

'[r]ecently the claim that the Sahara is advancing has been disputed. Evidence, based mainly on satellite images, does show annual changes resulting from variations in rainfall, but no permanent advance...[desert] boundaries are constantly changing as a result of variations in rainfall, and it is difficult to separate natural causes from human activity (e.g. is overgrazing a result of increased drought or increased human activity?)'(Waugh, 1994b, p. 49).

Waugh has a graph of rainfall in the region to show how a prolonged drought beginning in the early 1970s lent temporary plausibility to the fears of desertification (*ibid.*, p. 49). While this basic conclusion is believable,[3] a brief consideration of the graph soon leads to the impression that there is something strange about it. It features deviations from 'average rainfall for the period 1941-1992' in the sub-Sahara – but the sum of the deviations below the average shown greatly exceeds the total deviations above the average, a mathematical inconsistency. The result is to over-emphasise the frequency and severity of drought in the Sahara. While this does not alter Waugh's basic point, it is a

---

[3] Though incomplete; as Swift notes, 'a misreading of climatic variability is not enough to explain the tenacious hold of the received desertification narrative on the minds of politicians, civil servants, aid administrators and some scientists' (Swift, 1996, p. 86). The story also appealed to their ideological and institutional interests.

subtle example of how textbook presentations of environmental issues too often evidence a less-than-meticulous concern for the accuracy of the statistics they deploy.

Despite Waugh's discussion of the flaws in the desertification theory, he does not reject it outright. His text still features the flow-chart showing the classic causes of desertification: 'a combination of climatic changes (for example, decreased rainfall and global warming) with increased human activity and pressure upon the land (for instance, overgrazing, overcultivation and deforestation)' (*op. cit.*, p. 49). Instead of disavowing the desertification theory as misleading, Waugh asserts that maps of desertification need not be scrapped, only relabelled. Accordingly, his map locates places which, he claims, 'are at risk from desertification, *not* places where desertification has actually occurred' (p. 48). The evidence against desertification 'does not, of course, mean the risk has disappeared...Hopefully, the threat of desertification has increased people's awareness of the semi-arid lands as a fragile environment' (p. 49). The desertification myth will not die. In a strangely worded conclusion, Waugh states: 'Regardless of whether desertification is already a major hazard or whether it is a future risk, one thing is certain: increased desertification is likely, as with all environmental issues, to result from people's misuse of natural resources' (p. 49). Lack of evidence seems not to deter the desertification story. If not currently occurring, it is 'likely', or rather its increase is likely (implying that it is already in progress) – and that it is 'certain'!

Waugh's ambiguous account of the desertification problem illustrates a second reason, alongside National Curriculum requirements, for the durability of the desertification myth in textbooks. It frames the problems of African drought and famine in terms familiar to environmental discourse: they become a single global issue, one that requires extensive interventions by environmentally-concerned charitable organisations and governments in order to alter the destructive influence of humans on their fragile natural surroundings. In addition, textbook authors are partaking of a larger 'received wisdom' which portrays 'local land-use practices...as ill-adapted to contemporary socio-economic and demographic pressures' (Leach and Mearns (eds.), 1996, p. 5). The myth of desertification fits well with a neo-

Malthusian account of land degradation in Africa: population growth inevitably exceeds the 'carrying capacity' of the land, given its fragility and the primitive techniques of herding and cultivation practised by the indigenous people.

In fact, there are serious problems with the claim that overpopulation is a fundamental cause of land degradation, let alone desertification. There is evidence that, in Africa, extensive underpopulation may make it uneconomical for local agriculturalists to implement labour-intensive conservation measures which can better control soil loss and other forms of land degradation. In *More people, less erosion: environmental recovery in Kenya* (1994), Mary Tiffen, Michael Mortimore, and Francis Gichuki describe how rapid population growth has helped lead to changes in land-use techniques and a turn-around in soil conditions in the Machakos district from the 1930s to the early 1990s.

Learning to Patronise Peasants

Neo-Malthusian accounts of land degradation are not only simplistic and misconceived. They also paint an implicit picture of the people they describe as ignorant of the landscape they inhabit and unable to respond constructively to changes and challenges in the natural environment. In the standard textbook accounts of land degradation in Africa, 'rural people's ecological knowledge is notable mostly by its absence, silenced before it is investigated' (Leach and Mearns, 1996, p. 5). As many academics working on rural development issues have noted, these sorts of descriptions help justify intrusive interventions in the land-use practices of supposedly ignorant indigenous herders and farmers by outside 'experts' (*ibid.*, p. 20).

The way the 'solutions' to desertification and land degradation are portrayed in school textbooks too frequently follows along these very lines. In a box suggesting 'solutions to desertification', Jarman and Sutcliffe (in Ross (ed.), 1990, p. 38) feature a cartoon of a man in a jacket and shorts lecturing attentive 'ex-nomadic pastoralists' in traditional dress: 'You should settle down. I will show you how to grow crops with water from your new well. I will show you how to breed good quality cattle and how to look after your land in this delicate area.' The man in Western dress is standing under a 'protected tree', and behind him a fence walls off a replanted dune signposted 'no pastoralists'. Another text emphasises the need to plant 'trees, bushes and other vegetation'. The only obstacle here, apparently, is that the trees 'must be cared for while they are growing. It is difficult to change people's ways and stop them grazing their animals near the young trees, or cutting them down. People need educating in how to manage their land' (Punnett *et al.*, 1989, p. 39).

Historically, such efforts to teach indigenous people 'how to manage their land' have proved expensive and frequently counterproductive. For instance, campaigns to 'protect' trees often involve asserting state control over them, thereby disrupting indigenous patterns of property rights and leading to the resource's neglect. In Ethiopia, 'peri-urban plantations of eucalyptus declined sharply shortly after they were nationalised by the Derg [government]' (Hoben, 1996, p. 200). By contrast, people in the northern highlands of Ethiopia have integrated imported eucalyptus trees into their farming practices 'spontaneously without government extension program-mes...call[ing] into question the narrative that says peasants lack the ability or foresight to plant trees without environmental education, training, and access to subsidised seedlings from nurseries' (*ibid.*, p. 200).

Neither has the assumption often voiced in schoolbooks that nomadic pastoral practices are hopelessly unsuited to the environment proved correct. Daniel Brockington and Katherine Homewood argue that '[n]ew thinking in range ecology suggests that because of the resilience of savanna vegetation communities, they are not prone to collapse even under heavy grazing pressure. In semi-arid and arid environments it is rainfall rather than levels of grazing that determines productivity' (Brockington and Homewood, 1996, p. 96). What seems like 'overgrazing' is often a rational, and communally regulated, way of making full use of the short-lived opportunities presented by a landscape fraught with the ever-present risk of climatic change (*ibid.*, p. 97). Placing restrictions on herding practices may seem attractive from the point of view of concerned outsiders trying to root out the causes of 'desertification' and governments wishing to exert more control over mobile pastoralists. However, it is likely to be counterproductive, increasing grazing stress in the remaining areas accessible to herds, and reducing the pool of animal flesh that can be an important asset for consumption or sale in times of scarcity (Morris, 1995, p. 74).

Textbook authors propose similarly misguided interventionist solutions to the problem of soil erosion. They tend to frame their discussions very much from the point of view of a government 'planner' or an aid agency looking for a technological fix to the deficiencies of indigenous farming. One 1993 Geography GCSE question features a schematic diagram of a Sahelian farm complete with overgrazed vegetation and gulley erosion (see Figure 5). The following page presents a 'new method of farming being tried in parts of the Sahel', – a crescent-shaped stone wall designed to catch eroding earth on its way down a slope. Crops have been planted in the 'accumulated soil', and the reader is told to identify 'how the method shown...might help to overcome farming problems in the Sahel' (London East Anglian Group, 1993, p. 17). In fact, this idea is not new. It was among the methods implemented in a 'land reclamation' programme in Ethiopia during the 1980s, when aid agencies and the government had peasants build stone bunds and terraces. At the time locals complained, to no avail, that the bunds 'reduced arable land and harboured rodents'. Sure enough, later research showed that 'production on control plots was significantly higher under most crops and conditions than it was under any of the conservation measures' to which peasants had so objected (Hoben, 1996, p. 203). The aid effort, like so many of its kind, proved to be a vast waste of effort and resources.

Changing the Way We Educate about Africa

If outsiders have to bribe or coerce locals into taking up new crop species or land-use techniques, they are unlikely to be worthwhile, and will probably be abandoned as soon as the proj-

FIGURE 5:
Geography GCSE Exam showing new method of farming in the Sahel

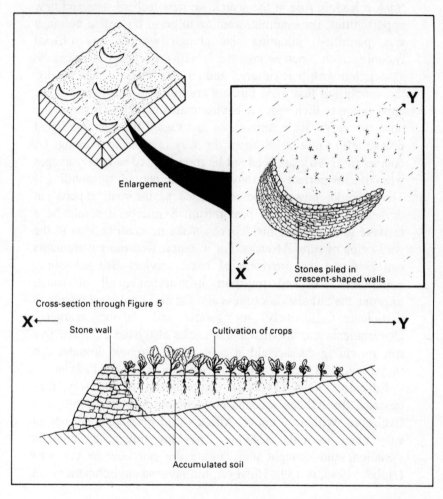

Enlargement

Stones piled in crescent-shaped walls

Cross-section through Figure 5

Stone wall

Cultivation of crops

Accumulated soil

Source: London Examinations, a division of Edexcel Foundation, GCSE Geography Paper, 14 June 1993, Syllabus D, Paper 2, p. 17.

ect to introduce them ends.[4]   Innovations that are truly valuable will be taken up voluntarily. Indeed, when allowed to, local people are constantly coming up with new ideas and techniques. The Kenyan farmers studied by Tiffen, Mortimore, and Gichuki 'took a leading role in the search for new technologies and new opportunities, for example, wanting to go in for coffee before it was permitted, adopting the plough without any official encouragement, perceiving the benefits of bench terraces in association with horticulture,' and so on (1994, p. 278). Really, the conclusion that local farmers are quick to innovate in ways appropriate to their specific environments is not at all surprising once we throw aside stereotypes and regard them as intelligent people who know a lot about the way they make a living. Of course, rural Africans need not be romanticised as noble savages who live in perfect harmony with their natural surroundings.[5] They should, however, be recognised as the real 'experts' in drylands cultivation and pastoralism. Similarly, it would be a mistake to infer that outsiders can make no contributions to the well-being of rural Africans. For instance, well-run governments can facilitate the provision of basic services like schooling, communications and transport infrastructure, all of which improve the circulation of ideas and the ability of rural people to participate effectively in goods and labour markets.[6] Governments and international agencies also have a constructive role providing disaster aid in cases of catastrophic drought. But they cannot tell rural people in Africa how to manage their land.

Educators need to revise comprehensively the way they describe the African savanna environment and the people who live there. Without a doubt, Africa's arid grasslands are not an easy place to make a living. They are fraught by climatic variation, and drought and famine are not new to the area (Hoben, 1996, p. 199). However, the savanna environment is not

---

[4]   In this sense, the recent and fashionable emphasis in educational literature on 'small-scale' as opposed to 'large-scale' rural development schemes misses the point. It is the pattern of implementing 'solutions' from above that is misguided.

[5]   This is the tack usually taken in descriptions of Amazonian Indians, for instance.

[6]   For a more comprehensive list of policy recommendations, see Tiffen *et al.*, 1996, pp. 277-84.

in a state of catastrophic decline. No permanent advance of the desert is occurring. African farmers and herders are not spoiling their land because of overpopulation and ignorance. These myths combine unsubstantiated environmental alarmism and implicit pejorative assumptions about Africans themselves. They must be replaced by a more realistic, more respectful view of the challenges and possibilities faced by Africans making a living from the land.

An Alternative Textbook Passage

The farmers and herders who live in the arid country south of the Sahara in Africa have to cope with a very difficult climate. In some years, the rains are good and there is plenty of food. At other times, droughts last for several years and can lead to widespread hunger. Often famine is brought on or made worse by war, by short-sighted government policies or by counter-productive land ownership arrangements.

In the past when there has been a long drought, observers have sometimes worried that 'desertification' is occurring, that local people are bringing about the advance of the desert. This has proved not to be the case, however; in fact, the edge of the desert moves back and forth over the course of many years depending on how much rain is falling.

In the past, international aid organisations and national governments in the Sahel have often blamed famines on the farming and herding practices of local people, and have tried to force or persuade them to adopt different schemes to change those practices. Generally these efforts have failed to improve the local people's standard of living, and often have done the opposite. This is because the locals had a better idea than the outside 'experts' of what ways of making a living suited the conditions in their area.

When farmers in the Sahel identify a new idea that looks like it works well, planting a new kind of tree or using a new method to control erosion, they tend to adopt it quickly themselves whether or not they are told to by their government or an international development expert. For this reason, it seems that governments and aid workers could better help by spreading information about new species and techniques rather than spending energy trying to get local people to adopt them. Governments and aid organisations can also assist in providing basic services that local people want, like education, and in providing food aid to regions threatened by starvation in times of prolonged drought.

5. Nature Conservation

Conservation might be called the grandfather of all environmental issues. It pre-dates, and, in all likelihood, will outlast more modern and probably more transient environmental campaign issues like the bioaccumulation of DDT or anthropogenic ozone thinning in the stratosphere. Conservation is perhaps the most important of all environmental challenges, since it involves fundamental human choices about how to co-exist with the huge diversity of non-human life on the planet.

The question of how human beings can best conserve natural ecosystems and habitats calls for non-formulaic, local answers. Accordingly, presenting conservation issues well in educational texts is a matter of representing as best as possible the real-world pressures that shape the way people use the living resources around them. Some accounts in the educational literature do this well, while others could afford to change their emphasis to tell a fuller, more representative story.

Since so much of the world's biodiversity and wildlife habitat is located in developing countries, it is natural that textbook authors devote plenty of space in their units on the developing world to conservation issues. More problematic is the assumption underlying some textbook discussions that the wild riches of the developing world can only be properly preserved by sequestering them in nature reserves, out of reach of greedy multinational corporations and mushrooming human populations in the Third World. The problem with this perspective is that if the conservation of the developing world's vast wild resources is to be extensive and effective, it must be undertaken by, and must benefit, the people who live there. The poorer populations of the world must be able to make a living from their natural surroundings. Otherwise, they will have little incentive to preserve them.

The sheer size of the Amazon rainforest and its frequent appearance in international environmental campaigns makes it the canonical example of threatened wildlife habitat in the developing world. This helps make Brazil one of the most popular Third World case studies in school geography texts. The wide range of textbook discussions of the Amazon region provides examples of both good and bad teaching about conservation.

Mapping Deforestation

The *Access to Geography 3* text contains several pages about Brazil and the Amazonian forest. After introducing some of the general characteristics of the forest ecosystem, the authors produce some alarming statistics about the rate of deforestation in the Brazilian Amazon. From 1975 to 1985, they claim, 12 per cent of the forest had been cleared, and in 1987 alone some 210,000 square kilometres were deforested (Kemp *et al.*, 1992, p. 15). These figures are almost certainly wrong: satellite surveys of the region indicate that over the decade from 1978 to 1987, average annual gross deforestation rates (excluding re-forestation, that is) ran at about $21,130 \text{ km}^2$, about one-tenth the rate of deforestation supposed to have taken place in 1987 (de Miranda, in Baden (ed.), 1994, p. 161). The figures cited by Kemp and his co-authors imply that in 1987 alone, about 6 per cent of the Brazilian tropical forest was lost,[1] while satellite data indicate that, in total, less than 10 per cent of the Amazonian forest had been cut by 1991 (*ibid.*, p. 162).

The *Access to Geography* text is not alone in featuring dubious statistics about the extent of deforestation. As part of the contemporary fashion for describing 'global' environmental problems, many textbook authors cite statistics for world-wide deforestation. From the map featured in David Waugh's *Key Geography for GCSE*, one would conclude that perhaps a third to a half of the world's tropical forests have been razed (Waugh, 1994b, p. 38). Another GCSE text claims that 'about half the world's forests have been removed during the last 30 years' (Barker *et al.*, 1994, p. 305). All of these statistics are highly suspect, and the last one is almost certainly false. Figures from the UN Food and Agriculture Organisation, for instance, suggest

---

[1] According to de Miranda, Legal Amazonia in Brazil has an area of $4,906,784 \text{ km}^2$, of which 70 per cent is tropical rain forest (de Miranda, 1994, p. 158).

that about 20 per cent of gross deforestation (that is, not counting forest regrowth) occurred in tropical forests from 1960 to 1990 (World Resources Institute, *et al.*, 1996, p. 209), while temperate and boreal forests were largely stable over the period. This is still a worrying statistic, although it is of a different order of magnitude from that cited by the other authors.

Even the FAO statistics are open to considerable doubt. For instance, the UN cites Guinea as a country where especially rapid deforestation has been taking place, and a FAO staff member is cited as stating that most of the forest changes in Africa 'occurred through the degradation of closed forest to open and fragmented forest and areas marked by shifting cultivation marked by short fallow periods' (*ibid.*, p. 211). Government and international experts surveying the border between forest and savanna in Guinea have often judged the green belts of vegetation around local villages to be 'relics of original primary forests',[2] when actually they are planted by the indigenous farmers of the region as part of a conscious land-management strategy. Reviewing a time-series of aerial photographs of the vicinity of Kissidougou in Guinea, supposedly an area of forest degradation, academics have concluded that changes in the region's vegetation have 'predominantly involve[d] increases in forest area' (Fairhead and Leach, in Leach and Mearns (eds.), 1996, p. 106-08). While this is only one local example, it makes one wonder how trustworthy the rest of the UN data are.

No doubt, our knowledge of the condition of global forests will markedly improve with the consistent application of satellite surveying techniques in coming years. While deforestation is not occurring on the scale suggested by the wilder textbook estimates, or even necessarily at the rate suggested in the FAO report, it is certainly worth worrying about. There is good reason to examine the habitat loss taking place, why it is happening and what measures should be taken to remedy it.

Beef, People, and Conservation in the Amazon

Returning to the example of deforestation in Brazilian Amazonia, the authors of the *Access to Geography* text rightly emphasise

---

[2] Notably, the FAO survey is 'based on data compiled from national inventory reports' (*op.cit.*, p. 204).

that 'large-scale development projects' have dominated the fate of the Amazon forest. If anything, they somewhat under-emphasise the contribution of government policies to deforestation in the region. The *Access to Geography* authors have a section on the 'Hamburger Connection': 'The beef in many hamburgers comes from Amazonian cattle ranches [that have government approval] – at the cost of the destruction of large areas of the fragile rainforest environment' (Kemp *et al.*, 1992, p. 21). The authors do not mention the fact that far from having simple 'government approval', the Brazilian government spent more than $1 billion in tax credits encouraging the establishment of cattle ranches in cleared forest areas from 1975-1986.

> 'These ranches have produced no more than 16% of their expected output. Many [ranchers] cleared the land, took the tax credit, but never raised a single joint of beef...In 1989 new tax credits were suspended...Cheap loans have been scaled down. And the rules that made land title conditional on forest clearance have been repealed' (Cairncross, 1991, p. 89).

Given the abject failure of the ranching scheme, it is unlikely that many of the hamburgers consumed by UK readers of Kemp's textbook come from Brazil. The lesson of the story is less that people in the developed world are eating their way through the Amazonian forest than that silly government schemes are often to blame for the environmental destruction taking place in the developing world.

A favourite theme of textbook discussions of deforestation in the Amazon involves drawing a distinction between the indigenous people of the forest who have lived in perfect harmony with the Edenic landscape from time immemorial and the more recent settlers in the area who invariably are unable to farm the land sustainably.[3] The authors of *Access to Geography* define 'indigenous' Indians as people 'who have always lived' in the area (Kemp *et al.*, 1992, p. 12). These 'true forest dwellers' practice 'shifting cultivation', a 'very balanced system of agriculture as the farmers are skilled in their choice of crops and

---

[3] See Candace Slater's article 'Amazonia as Edenic Narrative' in Cronon (1995), on this narrative pattern in most portrayals of the Amazon.

cultivation techniques'. By contrast, immigrants to the region practise 'a form of shifting cultivation called slash and burn' which involves completely exhausting the soil – destroying the forest and then moving on (*ibid.*, p. 20).

In fact, the distinction between 'shifting cultivation' and reckless-sounding 'slash and burn' agriculture is wholly rhetorical. Both immigrants and indigenous Indians cultivate the forest by cutting and burning the vegetation and then planting in the ash-fertilised soil. Whether or not the forest recovers depends on the intensity and duration of cultivation. Moreover, the idea that immigrants to Amazonia are incapable of farming sustainably in the forest is belied by the evidence. Where they have the incentive to settle down, immigrants to the Amazon have shown themselves able to set up sustainable farming in their areas of the forest (de Miranda, 1994, pp. 162-64). While government ranching subsidies and agricultural settlement schemes that encourage immigrants to clear new areas of forest progressively are undoubtedly effective means of reducing biodiversity in the Amazon, it is simply not true that the only people able to live in the forest without destroying the ecosystem are the indigenous Indians.

In his text on Amazonia, Waugh offers an example of how a textbook presentation can do better justice to the people who live in the forest. He comments that there are

'two extreme conflicts of interest in the rainforest. On the one hand there are those groups of people who wish to use the forest to make a quick profit. On the other, there are those who wish to protect the forest and leave it exactly as it is. Caught in the middle are the people who actually live there...They need to preserve the forest as well as being able to use its resources if they are to find work and improve their standard of living' (Waugh, 1994b, p. 42).

In an inset piece Waugh features a comment by a man called Emilio Sanchoma, who lives in the Amazon region of Peru. Sanchoma is quoted as saying:

'I was born in the rainforest and have lived here all my life. Like all rainforest people, I know how to harvest the forest sustainably... As rainforest people we are worried about our own way of life and about the future of the planet. We have been trying to find better ways of using the forest. In our area, the Palcazú Valley, the government has given us title to the land. We have set up the Yanesha Forestry Cooperative to log the forest on a sustainable basis' (*ibid.*, p. 43).

He gives a short description of the company's logging practices, which allow regrowth of the forest and minimum damage to the soil and surrounding vegetation during transport of the timber.

This passage is exemplary for a number of reasons. For one, it quotes an actual forest dweller, who states in his own words how he and his community manage to harvest the forest sustainably. This compares favourably with the *Access to Geography* text's use of a poem contrasting a mournful 'Song of Xingu Indian' and the rapacious voice of 'Amazonian Timbers, Inc.' (Kemp *et al.*, 1992, p. 17). The poem, which is written by Judith Nicholls (it is featured in the WWF sourcebook on 'environmental' assemblies, *The Green Umbrella*), gives no real voice to the people of the forest.[4] By contrast, Waugh's text gives a real, not an imagined, forest dweller the chance to speak about the way his community interacts with its environment.[5]

The quotation from Sanchoma emphasises that the permanent residents of the rainforest are likely to have a good sense of how to make a living there without totally devastating the local environment. In addition, the inset text mentions that the Peruvian government has given the community logging company title to the land. Waugh might have further developed the point by saying that if local people have secure rights to the

---

[4] Catherine McFarlane gives some very good advice for teaching about the environment in the Third World in the WWF Resource Pack for Primary Teachers. She advises teachers to check whether their teaching resources 'portray the people [in the developing world] as showing initiative and having power over their own lives' and whether they 'portray them sensitively, letting people speak for themselves' (McFarlane, in Smart (ed.), 1992, pp. 9-11). These guidelines point out what is problematic about featuring the Nicholls poem in a Geography text, and what is good about Waugh's inset on Emilio Sanchoma.

[5] Sanchoma's statement, which is drawn from a BBC/Longman text called the 'Global Environment', is evidently consciously directed at a Western audience – hence the constant emphasis on sustainability. But, while it may be part of a public relations exercise, and no doubt incompletely represents the complexities and failures of the Peruvian experiment, the statement *does* give a voice to an actual resident of the forest, and in a way that is relevant to ecological concerns of the textbook readers.

land where they live, they are more likely to make the expensive investments necessary to make use of resources sustainably. Readers could have been asked to consider how the Yanesha Forestry Cooperative's logging practices might have differed if the government had continued to hold title to the land, thus exposing the community to the possibility of eviction at any time.

Of course, conferring property rights to residents of the forest is not a fail-safe way of preserving the rainforest in the way Western conservationists wish. Even groups that sustainably harvest the plant riches of the forest often hunt the larger animals in their area to the point of local extinction (de Miranda, 1994, p. 163). Then again, no other conservation strategy is a panacea, either. Even the project of setting up Indian reserves designed to preserve traditional hunting and gathering practices as discussed in an Access to Geography unit entitled 'Assignment: Rescuing the Rainforest' (Kemp *et al.*, 1992, pp. 24-25) has fallen short of the expectations of environmentalists. The indigenous beneficiaries of the scheme discussed in the text, the Kayapó Indians, have engaged in illegal sales of timber from their reserve lands (Slater, 1995, pp. 121-24). In many cases, giving ownership of forest lands to the indigenous people may be a good idea from the point of view of historical equity, but Indians are no more immune to economic incentives than any other group of people.

Obviously there is no perfect way to preserve the natural riches of the rainforest while doing full justice to the needs and rights of forest residents. Some policies, like the Brazilian government's programme of ranching subsidies in the 1980s, are clearly expensive and silly, benefiting only rich landowners on the grab. Other measures, like David Waugh's recommendation that the 'international trade in such endangered hardwoods as mahogany' be reduced, may have a more ambiguous impact. While such a measure might check some rapacious logging companies, if applied in a universal way, it would also diminish the incentives for forest dwellers to cultivate or protect the endangered trees on lands that they own. Similarly, how would setting up national parks and forest reserves, another suggestion of Waugh's (Waugh, 1994b, p. 43), affect the people who live inside the reserve region?

Nature reserves of some sort, perhaps with funding from conservation organisations that can financially represent the interests of the developed world in the wildlife of the Amazon, no doubt have a crucial role in helping preserve the Amazonian forest. However, the forest is too vast and is the home of too many people to be turned into a single big wildlife park. At the least, governments in the Amazon region can avoid expensively subsidising the destruction of the forest. At best, good government policies that cost agricultural expansion into virgin areas and encourage the replanting of degraded areas of forest can give people an incentive to invest in the sustainable exploitation of the forest.

It is perhaps less important for educators to offer specific 'solutions' to conservation dilemmas than it is for them to explore the ways in which different conservation methods distribute the costs and benefits of conserving wildlife and wildlife habitats. In particular, textbooks could put more emphasis on policies that go beyond the simple legal sequestration of wildlife habitat and instead try to make it worthwhile for local people to preserve the wild resources around them.

Conservation in Africa: Learning to Ask Better Questions

Textbook accounts that emphasise the importance of simply creating game sanctuaries often miss the costs imposed by wildlife reserves on local residents. In a discussion of game reserves in Africa, 'Safari or sanctuary', one set of authors expresses concern over the way in which tourist facilities in parks 'are artificial to the natural savanna ecosystem', and provides an illustration of enthusiastic white tourists besieging a group of bewildered animals who have come to drink at a waterhole (Kemp et al., 1992, pp. 38-39). They show further concern for the constraints put by humans on protected animals in a discussion of the control methods used to deal with the burgeoning lion populations in one Namibian park. The text contrasts the park management's 'scientific' contraception programme for the lions with the preference by 'farmers outside the park' for 'game management by shooting'. They conclude this section by commenting that, despite the success of the contraception programme, 'one question people ask is whether we have a right to control wild animals in this way' (*ibid.*, p. 39).

This extraordinary concern for the rights of wildlife to an undisturbed, unconstrained existence misses many of the more pressing problems associated with African wildlife reserves. For one, the programme of contraception was probably an extraordinarily expensive way of controlling the lion population. Choosing to shoot stray lions may not have been as ethically sensitive a choice as neutering them (although it mystifies me why it is a less 'scientific' approach), but it probably would have discouraged the rest of the lions from going into inhabited areas, and might have saved the game reserve enough money to buy more land for habitat conservation purposes.

Only people who do not make a living in the vicinity of wildlife reserves have the luxury of questioning whether or not human beings have the right to control wild animals. The proximity of wildlife imposes significant costs on herders and farmers living in the vicinity. In many of Africa's wetter areas, wild animals harbour the trypanosome parasite that kills cattle and causes deadly 'sleeping sickness' in humans. Having a game reserve nearby can bring lethal disease. In drier areas, the managers of wildlife reserves often exclude pastoralists from their traditional grazing grounds. As the *Access to Geography* text itself notes, 'many poachers are local people, often pastoralists whose traditional grazing areas have been lost due to the creation of national parks and game reserves' (Kemp *et al.*, 1992, p. 40). Another text states that Masai herders 'use the Ngorongoro Crater alongside the wild animals. The Masai are forbidden to graze their cattle in the Serengeti Park itself, because they would eat the vegetation the wild animals need' (Punnett *et al.*, 1989, pp. 52-53).[6]

---

[6] This assumption may be somewhat misplaced. In the Ngorongoro, where wild animals and pastoralists co-exist, 'it is argued that wildlife competes successfully with livestock, and that the pastoralists rather than the animals are on the retreat' (Brockington and Homewood, 1996, p. 97).

Given all of the costs that the creation of national parks imposes on local people, textbooks should devote attention to the ways in which reservations can be made to benefit them in recompense. Not only is this important from the point of view of fairness, it also matters for the long-term success of wildlife preservation itself. Conservation in the teeth of local opposition is an expensive and oppressive business. This is the broad thrust of the latest thinking about conservation (see, for instance, Edwards, 1995, p. 223ff). Recently, some park managers in Africa have worked out agreements with local pastoralists to grant them shared use of the grazing land. Outside the reserves, 'extension work, adult education, and projects channelling wildlife revenues to local communities are encouraging wildlife to be viewed as a valuable resource' (Leach and Mearns, 1996, p. 97).

In another development, some individual entrepreneurs and communities have tried to make wildlife conservation into a business venture. The *Access to Geography* text contains a small mention of 'wildlife ranching': 'Phil Tilby, who manages the pilot ranch at Arthi, 40km from Nairobi, argues that exploiting animals for profit is the most feasible route to wildlife conservation' (Kemp *et al.*, 1992, p. 41). The idea of passing on the benefits of wildlife conservation to communities has also found its way into a recent GCSE exam.

A 1995 GCSE question features a new programme in Zimbabwe which devolves decisions over wildlife from central government officials to village councils. The CAMPFIRE project is introduced rather cautiously; the authors note the economic difficulties of villages in the Beitbridge area of southern Zimbabwe before 1969, and the fact that they earned some income from safari hunting.

'Although the idea of rich trophy hunters killing animals is unpleasant to many people, the government of Zimbabwe feels that if it is controlled carefully, it will bring in more money to the country. The government has set up CAMPFIRE projects where the money earned from safari hunting comes back to the people in villages like those in the Beitbridge area.'

The text describes how the villagers spent the earnings by individual household, and also collectively, on education and a

74

maize-grinding mill. It also comments that villagers chose to regulate the annual kill of animals, and leads the reader to the conclusion that this decision assures local people a perpetual stream of income. The examiners comment that the 'project has given the villagers the opportunity to manage the wildlife and the income produced', and ask whether they think the scheme has helped the villagers (London East Anglian Group, 1995a, pp. 24-25).

The examiners cover the basics of the scheme well. Although they could have emphasised more strongly that CAMPFIRE gives local people an incentive to bear the costs of having game animals living in their vicinity, the authors of the question do put across the fundamental way in which the arrangement benefits both villagers and wildlife. One hopes that exams and textbooks will feature an increasing number of such examples illustrating the fact that the chance to derive economic benefit from the wild can make conservationists of the people who are closest to the animals and plants in question and so are best equipped to husband them.[7]

The challenges of conservation in the Third World are much more complex than a simple choice between nature and economic development, as is often portrayed in textbooks. At present, educational texts feature countless exercises asking whether the governments of developing countries should 'develop' their natural resources or preserve them,[8] a debate which most schoolchildren (and textbook authors) in the developed world have long since resolved in favour of nature. Ultimately, the question as it is posed is a sterile one. Children should be taught to think about how conservation and sustainable resource use on the one hand and economic progress on the other can coexist. If government policies do not actively subsidise

---

[7] Of course, people almost always take some steps to conserve the natural resources that they depend upon. The point of these latter schemes is to lead them to extend and adapt their stewardship practices to species and habitats they would not otherwise choose to conserve.

[8] This baldly dichotomised question is brought up time and again in slightly varied versions. For examples, see Foskett et al., 1987, p. 61; Kemp et al., 1992, pp. 24-25 and p. 93; Waugh, 1994b, p. 43; University of London Examinations and Assessment Council, 1995c, pp. 18-19.

environmental destruction, and if they encourage institutions that allow local people to reap the benefits of sustainable use and wildlife conservation, economic development can go hand-in-hand with a non-destructive use of the land and its resources. To the extent that these sorts of policies can be achieved, human prosperity can flourish alongside a thriving and diverse non-human world.

An Alternative Textbook Passage

We human beings have lots of neighbours on our planet. Millions of different kinds of plants and animals inhabit the land and the oceans, each species with its own distinct and fascinating way of living in its surroundings. How can people conserve as much as possible of this rich natural heritage while making a living from the Earth for themselves?

One way of conserving natural habitats is for the government to set aside certain areas as nature reserves and parks. This has led to the preservation of large areas of habitat in the developed and developing world. Sometimes, though, this strategy has involved great hardship for the people using the land at the time the government sets it aside as natural habitat. In Africa, for instance, many pastoralists and farmers have been pushed off the land during the creation of reserves. The wild animals who inhabit the new reserves can also cause hardship for local people nearby when they eat or trample crops, prey on domesticated herds, or, in wetter areas, spread sleeping sickness, which can be fatal to cattle and people. It's not always easy living next to wildlife!

For this reason, many conservationists have begun to emphasise the importance of looking for ways in which protecting animals and their habitats can be made to benefit local people. Some of the money paid by tourists visiting nature reserves can be turned over to local communities. Park authorities can share grazing land with nearby pastoralists. In some cases, local villages that win the right to take revenues from game hunters and tourists have decided to set up their own game reserves as a way of bringing money into their communities.

As this last example illustrates, people in developed countries can be very important in making it worthwhile for the poorer residents of the developing world to conserve wildlife habitat. Often they are the tourists or hunters who pay for the chance to enjoy the wildlife they cannot see at home. Conservation organisations funded by people in the developed world can pay for habitat preservation in the Third World.

6. Conclusion

The canon of environmental issues as it is currently presented in school textbooks needs revising. At present, children learn an inadequate account of the problems of resource scarcity. They are taught that supplies of various 'non-renewable' resources are set to 'run out' at some fairly specific date in the future. A more economically sophisticated lesson would help them understand how the scarcity of a non-renewable resource expresses itself in its price, which in turn prompts consumers and producers to compensate for the commodity's scarcity, conserving on consumption of it, going to greater length to search out reserves of it, or substituting for it with cheaper alternatives.

Acid rain is another inadequately taught topic in the environmental curriculum. Many textbook authors adhere to the old story of acid rain as the leveller of forests and shame of Britain, the 'dirty man of Europe'. This account needs to be substituted with a more scientifically accurate rendition of the problem: to wit, acid rain's effects on forests, while harmful in the long term, are more subtle and less acutely lethal than once was feared; the acidification of aquatic ecosystems is often the fault of land-use practices as well as of acid rain itself; and Britain should not suffer the primary blame for Scandinavian acidification, since only a small proportion of the acid precipitation that falls in Norway and Sweden can be traced to British sources. This more accurate representation of the problems of acid rain can lead pupils to a fuller appreciation of the policy dilemmas posed by acid rain.

The gulf between academic science and textbook renditions of environmental problems also shows itself in teaching about global warming. Here the problem is that textbooks tend to underestimate scientific uncertainty over the likely path of climate change in the future. Some authors present at face value predictions taken from models whose forecasts fail even to predict the present. Textbook accounts also tend to understate the consequences of efforts to halt anthropogenic emissions of CO_2,

78

and so misrepresent the sacrifices involved in acting to pre-empt possible climate change. Children deserve access to a more honest account of the uncertainties and hard choices involved in the issue.

Desertification is one of the most troubling environmental crisis issues. Its history is marred by poor science, political coercion, and, when traced back to its colonial past, racism. In short, the advance of the desert as a result of a neo-Malthusian cycle of overpopulation and improvident land use is myth and should be excised from the curriculum. In place of the desertification story, pupils should learn about the real difficulties faced by peasants farming arid regions – both of a climatic nature and in the form of oppressive government bureaucracies. Geography textbooks show a marked reluctance to criticise the shortcomings of Third-World governments, which is a shame since they often end up implicitly slandering the people subject to those governments instead.

By comparison, textbook accounts about conservation tend to be better. The chief criticism that can be levelled against some of them is the inadequate attention given to the local people in developing countries who often bear the brunt of government efforts to conserve wildlife habitat. These authors could afford to bring their stories about conservation in line with recent thinking in conservation circles by emphasising the importance of trying to harmonise conservation efforts in the Third World with the interests of the people who make a living in or near protected habitats.

The sort of criticisms that apply to environmental narratives in educational texts are also pertinent to most public presentations of the same issues. School texts must simplify for their young audience, but in fact popular accounts of environmental issues usually contain simplifications that are no less drastic. The reasons for this can largely be traced to the political origins of environmental issues. They are born of the environmental movement's desire to identify nature's ills and their remedies in a straightforward and urgent way that is readily communicable and serves as a basis for political action. Environmental issues are the outcomes of a rhetorical history, and they show it. Thus, a textbook map shows Central Europe and Scandinavia to be suffering the ravages of acid rain while France and other Southern European countries experiencing comparable rates of sulphur deposition apparently escape unscathed. The map makes sense from the point of view of the political history of acid rain, if not on the basis of the physical mechanisms involved.

This is not to say, of course, that every element of the environmental canon is simply politicised mythology. Acid rain does modify forest ecosystems, and acidify some soils, decimating nearby aquatic life. Human-induced global warming is a real possibility. Often the concerns raised by environmentalists are valid and their aims laudable. But it is also not true that any degree of distortion in presenting environmental problems can be excused on the grounds that the cause is just. Any such view is arrogant and historically misinformed. Misguided environmental policy made on the basis of inaccurate stories can be costly in economic and human terms.

While, of course, environmental education cannot be held responsible for the shortcomings of policy, it does reflect the flaws of wider environmentalist discourse. Most school texts do too little to provide pupils with the most up to date information possible on environmental issues. Finding this sort of information can be difficult, and often requires forays into the academic literature. Since teachers cannot possibly have enough time to do this on every issue, textbook and exam authors should take the task upon themselves.

Perhaps more seriously, educational texts all too often use evidence in a naïve and broadly demonstrative way, making it an unexamined adjunct to a set narrative. Educational authors need to think harder about the evidence they use, and to teach children to do the same. Learning to be demanding with evidence, to ask difficult questions about its inner consistency, its origins, and its implications, is a crucial lesson that we must constantly learn and re-learn, and that might as well begin in school.

People with all different sorts of ideological agendas often see schoolchildren as uniquely receptive targets of indoctrination, either with the wrong or the right point of view. I think this underestimates the amount of forgetting and re-learning that we generally do throughout our lives. It would be too much to claim for environmental education either the power to 'save the Earth' or to turn children into brainwashed environmental activists, as some conservatives no doubt fear. All the same, improvements in environmental education could help equip children to be more savvy, humane environmentalists as adults.

References

Official Publications

Department of Education and Science (DES) (1991a): *Geography in the National Curriculum* (England), London: HMSO.

Department of Education and Science and the Welsh Office (DES) (1991b): *Science in the National Curriculum*, London: HMSO.

National Acidic Precipitation Assessment Program (NAPAP) (1990): *Acidic Deposition: State of Science and Technology.*

World Resources Institute, UNEP, UNDP and World Bank (1996): *World Resources 1996-7: A Guide to the Global Environment.*

Monographs

Ackerman and Hassler (1981): *Clean Coal/Dirty Air*, New Haven: Yale University Press.

Anderson, T., and Leal D. (1991): *Free Market Environmentalism*, San Francisco: Pacific Research Institute for Public Policy.

Baden, J. (ed.) (1994): *Environmental Gore: A Constructive Response to 'Earth in the Balance'*, San Francisco: Pacific Research Institute for Public Policy.

Bailey, R. (ed.) (1995): *The True State of the Planet*, New York: The Free Press.

Balling, R. Jr. (1992): *The Heated Debate: Greenhouse Predictions Versus Climate Reality*, San Francisco: Pacific Research Institute for Public Policy.

-------- (1995): 'Global Warming: Messy Models, Decent Data, and Pointless Policy', in Bailey (ed.), *The True State of the Planet*.

Bate, R. (1996): 'An Economist's Foreword', in Emsley (ed.), *The Global Warming Debate*.

Brockington, D. and Homewood, K. (1996): 'Wildlife, Pastoralists & Science', in Leach and Mearns (ed.), *The Lie of the Land*.

Cairncross, F. (1991): *Costing the Earth*, London: Random House.

Cairncross, F. (1995): *Green, Inc. Guide to Business and the Environment*, London: Earthscan Publications.

Cronon, W. (1995): *Uncommon Ground: Toward Reinventing Nature*, London: Norton.

East, J., Hill P., and Rue R. (1994): *Eco-Sanity: A Common-sense Guide to Environmentalism*, The Heartland Institute, Madison Books.

Edwards, S. R. (1995): 'Conserving Biodiversity: Resources for Our Future', in Bailey (ed.), *The True State of the Planet*.

Emsley, J. (ed.) (1996): *The Global Warming Debate: The Report of the European Science and Environment Forum*, Bournemouth: Bourne Press.

Hoben, A. (1996): 'The Cultural Construction of Environmental Policy', in Leach and Mearns (ed.), *The Lie of the Land*.

Howells, G. (1995): *Acid Rain and Acid Waters*, 2nd edition, E. Honvood.

Idso, S. (1996): 'Plant Responses to Rising Levels of Atmospheric Carbon Dioxide', in Emsley (ed.), *The Global Warming Debate*.

Leach, M., and Mearns, R. (eds.) (1996): *The Lie of the Land: challenging received wisdom on the African environment*, London: James Currey Ltd.

Lindzen, R. (1994): 'The Origin and nature of the Alleged Scientific Consensus', in Baden, J. (ed.), *Environmental Gore.*

Michaels, P., and Knappenberger, P. (1996) 'Evidence from the Scandinavian Tree Line since the Last Ice Age', in Emsley, J. (ed.), *The Global Warming Debate.*

de Miranda, E. (1994): 'Tropical Rainforests - Myths and Realities', in Baden, J. (ed.), *Environmental Gore.*

Moore, S. (1995): 'The Coming Age of Abundance', in Bailey, R. (ed.), *The True State of the Planet.*

Morris, J. (1995): *The Political Economy of land Degradation: Pressure Groups, Foreign Aid and the Myth of Man-Made Deserts*, London: Institute of Economic Affairs Environment Unit.

Slater, C. (1995): 'Amazonia as Edenic Narrative' in Cronon, W. (ed.), *Uncommon Ground: Towards Reinventing Nature.*

Swift, J. (1996): 'Desertification: Narrative, Winners and Losers', in Leach and Mearns (ed.), pp. 73-90.

Tiffen, M., Mortimore, M. and Gichuki, F. (1994): *More People, Less Freedom: Environmental Recovery in Kenya*, Chichester: Wiley & Sons.

The World Wide Fund for Nature (1991): *The Green Umbrella*, Gland, Switzerland: WWF.

Educational publications and videos

Barker, M., Jones A., and Millican, C. (1994): *Longman Revise Guide: GCSE/Key Stage 4 Biology*. Harlow: Longman.

Barton, D. (1993): *Longman Revise Guide. GCSE/Key Stage 4 Science*, 2nd edition, Harlow: Longman.

Foskett, R., Kemp N., and MacLean (eds.) (1987): *Geography for GCSE: People in the Rural Landscape*, London: Macdonald Educational.

Johnson, K., Adamson S., and Williams, G. (1995a): *Spotlight Science 9*, Cheltenham: Stanley Thornes.

Johnson, K, Adamson S., and Williams, G. (1995b): *Spotlight Science 9: Teacher's Guide*, Cheltenham: Stanley Thornes.

Kemp, R., Sims, T., and Stevens, A. (1995): *Access to Geography 3: Key Stage 3*. Oxford: Oxford University Press.

Marsden, B. and V. (1995): *Oliver and Boyd Geography. Book 4*, Harlow: Longman.

McElroy, M. and Sadler, J. (1994): *Longman Revise Guide. GCSE/Key Stage 4 Chemistry*, 2nd edition, Harlow: Longman.

Punnett, N., Webber, P. and Murray, S. (1988): *The Developed World: The Geography Project 2*, Cheltenham: Stanley Thornes.

------ (1989): *The Developing World: The Geography Project 3*, Cheltenham: Stanley Thornes.

Ross, S., (ed.) (1990): *Longman Coordinated Geography*, Harlow: Longman.

Shell Film and Video Unit (1991): 'Climate of Concern'.

Smart, J., (ed.) (1992): *'My World': A Resource Pack for Primary Teachers*, Gland: World Wide Fund for Nature.

Waugh, D. (1994a): *Key Geography for GCSE: Book 1*, Cheltenham: Stanley Thornes.

------ (1994b): *Key Geography for GCSE: Book 2*, Cheltenham: Stanley Thornes.

Wright, D. (1993): *Philip's Environment Atlas for Children*, in association with the World Wide Fund for Nature, 2nd edition, Oxford: Heinemann Publishers.

GCSE exam papers by the University of London Examinations and Assessment Council.

Geography

(London East Anglian Group): Monday 3 June 1991 – Morning, Geography (Syllabus A), Paper 2.

Thursday 6 June 1991 – Afternoon, Geography (Syllabus B), Paper 2.

Thursday 4 June 1992 – Afternoon, Geography (Syllabus A) 3E: Energy (Optional Paper).

14 June 1993, Geography Paper 2 (Syllabus D).

Friday 16 June 1995a – Morning Paper 1.

Friday 16 June 1995b – Morning: Geography A, Paper 3E – Energy

Science

Monday 5 June 1995c – Afternoon. Double Award (Combined): Paper 21 (part 04) and Biology A: Paper 21 (Part 03).

An American Perspective on Environmental Literacy:

A New Goal For Environmental Education

Dr Jo Kwong

1. Introduction

Criticism of environmental education has mounted steadily during the past two years, with critics arguing that environmental education efforts are largely:

1) doomsday oriented;

2) fear generating;

3) geared towards activism; and

4) devoid of science teaching.

While these criticisms may be well-founded, they fail to get at the heart of the 'environmental education problem'. In essence, the problem is that we have mounted an educational campaign aimed at turning our nation's school children into environmentalists. This aim is founded on the belief that environmentalism leads to environmental literacy. However, we will fail to achieve environmental literacy – knowledge of natural and environmental systems and application of that knowledge towards problem solving – if we rely on *environmentalists*, rather than *educators*, to provide the 'teaching'. We need to refocus our perspective by teaching young children the basic sciences, outdoor education, conservation, and in later years, integrating this knowledge with problem solving skills. Further, we need to distinguish between decision-making based on knowledge and slogan-generated advocacy, in order to achieve environmental literacy.

This paper critiques environmental education as it is currently taught in the US, illustrates the tremendous influence of environmentalism upon children, and offers an alternative model for achieving environmental literacy.

Environmentalists are Advocates, not Educators

In this era of environmental awareness, everyone from the corporate chief executive officer to the corner grocer to the Tupperware salesperson, works hard to demonstrate their commitment to the environment. But we have been careless in using and defining the term 'environmentalist'. Almost everyone prefers a healthy, clean environment over a dirty, ailing one. Most are willing to take common sense actions to foster a healthier environment: picking up litter, reducing energy use, properly disposing of toxic waste, recycling materials that can be efficiently re-used, and so on. In this sense, everyone is an 'environmentalist', making the label essentially redundant. When we do use it, however, the label most appropriately describes *professional* environmentalists.

Professional environmentalists derive their living from advocating specific actions and processes. In the USA, the employees of the National Wildlife Federation, Sierra Club, Greenpeace and the Natural Resources Defense Council, are but a few examples of professional environmentalists. These groups have clear positions on virtually every environmental issue. Most are opposed to oil drilling in Alaska's Arctic National Wildlife Refuge, heartily endorse legislation requiring recycled content for manufacturing processes, advocate greater governmental control and ownership of environmental resources, argue for the elimination of CFCs from the economy, and warn that acid rain, ozone depletion, and global warming rank high on the list of impending global disasters.

These are not unbiased positions. In fact they are clear advocacy positions. And advocates for particular causes make poor teachers (unless you want to learn how to be an advocate). Professional environmentalists enter the classroom with a preconceived notion of right and wrong. Their job is to get the children to agree with their positions, not to provide an unbiased account from which children can make informed decisions

The job of environmental educators, on the other hand, is to provide an information base and foster critical thinking. Repetitive slogans to 'save the world', 'save the rainforest', or that 'green is beautiful', do little to foster sound comprehension with an eye towards problem solving.

Yet, professional environmentalists are affecting current environmental education. They produce and disseminate materials for teachers. They serve as guest presenters in the classroom, armed with advocacy lessons. They supply materials to the US Environmental Protection Agency's Office of Environmental Education, which serves as a clearinghouse for green educational materials. The results have been predictably disappointing. In the USA, and presumably elsewhere, we are producing a nation of 'doomsday kids' or 'eco-kids' – children who can tell you what (they think) is right and wrong, but who are woefully ignorant of the reasons why these might be so. In essence, we are teaching our children what to think, rather than how to think. They are, quite simply, environmentally illiterate.

2. A Critique of Environmental Education

Earlier this spring, I picked up my five-year-old twin daughters from nursery, along with two of their friends. Knowing that a guest presenter had come to discuss recycling, I was ready for battle. As I drove away from the school, I asked, 'What did you learn in school today?'

Four pairs of eyes looked blankly at me until daughter Jessica said: 'Nothing.' I said: 'But I thought someone came and talked to you about recycling today. Can anyone tell me what recycling is?'. A resounding chorus of 'NO!' from the back seat. Pressing on, I asked 'Well, is recycling something we should do? ... is it a good thing?' The chorus now shouted 'Yes!'. 'Now wait a minute, kids,' I said. 'If you don't know what recycling is, how can you be so sure we should do it?' Daughter Asia, recognising their logical inconsistency, moved to answer the question. 'I think you make furniture or something out of it.'

I could only guess that perhaps someone mentioned the production of plastic park benches from recycled materials. Of course, it's difficult to reconstruct the thought pattern of a 5-year-old. Yet one thing was clear: The children were taught that recycling is good and they should do it, well before they could even imagine what recycling actually means.

This story is not at all unusual. Parents are increasingly complaining about the environmental dogma children are receiving. And with good reason. Even a cursory review of environmental educational literature reveals a number of unsettling trends. Environmental education:

- is often based on emotionalism, myths, and misinformation;

- is often issue-driven, rather than information driven;

- typically fails to teach children about basic economics or basic decision-making processes, relying instead on mindless slogans;

- often fails to take advantage of lessons from nature, and instead preaches socially- or politically-correct lessons;

- is unabashedly devoted to activism and politics, rather than knowledge and understanding;

- teaches that man is an intrusion on the earth, and at times, evil; and

- extends beyond the school systems and traditional 'educators' and well into the realm of toys, colouring books, food products, and other areas.

The Literature of Despair

According to *Environmental Almanac 1994*, 'books with environmental themes are well represented among more than 81,000 estimated children's books in print'. A quick look through the children's nature section of my local public library illustrates prevalent themes and teachings among environmental educators: *Saving Planet Earth, The Kids' Earth Handbook, Earth Book for Kids: Activities to Help Heal the Environment, Teaching Kids to Love the Earth, Save the Earth: An Action Handbook for Kids, The Kids' Environment Books: What's Awry and Why*, or *Kid Heroes of the Environment: Simple Things Real Kids are Doing to Save the Earth*. One wonders how the authors continue to come up with unique ways to combine 'save' and 'earth'.

As I maintain throughout this paper, teaching children about nature and the environment is one thing; motivating them to 'save' the Earth is another. Consider typical introductions to environmental texts. In *Saving Planet Earth*, the opening paragraph tells children: 'in the last 200 years, human beings have been polluting and damaging the planet so severely that now the very future of life on Earth may be in danger. How have we engineered such a terrible thing in so short a time?'. In *Save the Earth*, an 'action handbook for kids to save the Earth', author Betty Miles begins by describing the 'fragile' earth. 'The Earth's grave problems, like overflowing landfills, oil spills and acid rain, are huge and discouraging.' The emphasis on the irreversible is evident. The chapter on land, for example, speaks of wanton destruction:

'Farm land is being destroyed – sometimes irreversibly...Cutting down the Earth's old-growth forests destroys thousands of acres of land each day. This destruction may never be reversed...land is destroyed by the wars that rage over it...'

On that ever popular theme of rainforest preservation, Miles writes: '...today these ancient rain forests are being cut down and burned at a rate so fast that scientists predict all of them will vanish within a century. Once it has been destroyed, a rain forest is gone forever. It will never come back' (Miles, 1991, p.64).

This strategy of despair has its costs. Some educators, at least, are recognising its toll on children. In 1993, the topic on the Internet's KIDFORUM was 'Environment-2093' (www.kid-link/KIDFORUM). Students were asked to project themselves one hundred years into the future and describe the environmental shape of their communities. 150 students from Denmark, Iceland, Germany, and the US participated. Moderator Joanne Wilson expected pessimistic forecasts, but when nearly half the students drew doomsday pictures, she was surprised and alarmed at the hopelessness evident in many of the students' words. Wilson asked other KIDFORUM adults: 'Does it concern any of you to see how dark the future is in the eyes of so many of these children?' Some of the responses included:[1]

'That was the first thing I noticed when my students were writing. It really bothered me.'

'We encourage our kids to take action..., but we also terrorize them with the daily news that we read.'

---

[1] Taken from 1993 discussion on the topic of eco-despair noticed among youth on KIDLINK computer network.

'Are we teaching powerlessness when our hope/intent is to teach empowerment/responsibility?'

'Yes, the sense of doom pervading most environmental scenarios gives me pause. The sense of inevitability and powerlessness implicit in the kids' postings may indicate that the seeds of cynicism are planted early on.'

Philosophy professor Stephen Hicks suspects the remnants from despair are in fact learned early on and are carried over to his college students.

'My college freshmen classes are regularly populated by young adults who are convinced that no solutions are possible and so it's useless to try, or who are so desperate for answers that they latch on to the first semi-plausible solution they encounter and become close-minded. Both apathy and dogmatism are defense mechanisms against feeling that you are living in a hostile world whose problems are too big for you to handle. And these are attitudes children often acquire early in their school careers' (Hicks, 1991).

Ginny Moore Kruse, director of the Cooperative Children's Book Center at the University of Wisconsin and author of *Children's Books in Print, 1993*, refers to environmental issues books as the 'literature of despair.' She asks: 'How can children feel excitement about the environment when they're introduced through bleak, heavy-handed issue books that harp on global warming and habitat destruction?' (*Environmental Almanac*, 1994).

Joanne Wilson addressed this specific concern in an adult KIDLINK forum called 'Kidleader'. Participants, primarily teachers, analysed their part in robbing students of youthful idealism. They generated ideas for teaching students creative responses based on positive, responsible actions towards the environment.

Not all teachers, however, share the concern over eco-despair. Thomas Holt writes: 'Many of those who shape the environmental education curriculum believe that their purpose is not to weigh conflicting facts, values, and theories, but to instill a sense of crisis'. Holt quotes the Wildlife Center of Virginia's Ed Clark, who said, 'Understanding that the world is going to hell in a handbasket is half of environmental education' (Holt, 1991).

Judging from reviews of kids' writings, this perspective of environmental education has been successful. A Virginia newspaper, *The Culpeper Star-Exponent,* asked children: 'What responsibility do we have to Mother Earth?' LaShonda Newman responded: 'The Earth would be a bad place to live if we didn't have children like me to keep it clean.' Andrew Standley said, 'If you don't keep it clean the Grand Canyon will become a landfill and the whole earth will be destroyed by litter, trash and all that stuff.'[2]

In a 1995 Earth Day Photo and Essay Contest, sponsored by the Delaware Earth Day Committee in conjunction with the *Delaware Coast Press* newspaper, children shared their concerns. Elizabeth Conner, the first place elementary school winner, said she is going to 'teche [teach] my sister to save the Earth.' Second place elementary school winner, Abigail Sadler, wrote about her ideas to save the Earth:'...recycle, ride bikes, make less factories, stop polluting and stop spraying agricultural crops' with 'some kind of spray.' 'If we don't do something now, we won't have a planet!' (*Delaware Coast Press,* 12 April 1995).

Emotionalism, Hype, and Misinformation

The eco-despair has been bolstered by emotionalism and misinformation. Any sampling of green materials for children reveals a mine field of errors, misstatements, and half truths.

For example, global warming, one of the most extensively-covered issues, has been widely taught as if it is a sinister process resulting from greedy human behaviour. Materials make little mention of doubts, controversy, or conflicting perspectives regarding alternative hypotheses. The final impression is that catastrophic global warming is occurring and only drastic action can reverse the effects.

In reality, the Earth's warming is a natural, necessary phenomenon. Essential for the existence of life forms on earth, greenhouse gases, such as carbon dioxide, raise the average temperature to about 60 degrees Fahrenheit. What scientists

---

[2] 'Issue: Environment', *Culpeper Star-Exponent,* Culpeper, VA, 26 February 1994.

disagree on is whether increased carbon dioxide from coal burning and auto emissions will change the climate. The understanding is so vague that in the mid- to late-1970s scientists predicted we were headed for a disaster via global *cooling*. Yet, to read the accounts in textbooks, the impacts of global warming are eminent.

The DC Heath text *Earth Science: The Challenge of Discovery* has a section labeled 'Slowing Global Warming' which notes 'Humans are causing climate change faster than they can find out how climate works' (Snyder *et al.*, 1991). The Scott Foresman textbook, *History and Life*, describes the effects of global warming by stating that 'major port cities, such as New York, Buenos Aires, and Hong Kong, would be submerged beneath the sea' (Wallbank, 1993).

A Prentice Hall *Science Gazette* article describes the consequences of warming of the Earth with photographs of houses falling into the sea and a 1930s dust bowl farm. The text notes that warming in the polar regions could melt the ice and increase sea level by 'as much as seven or eight meters!' Severe drought would occur in the western United States and 'farms might have to be abandoned because of lack of water'. In other places, more rain will fall, but this is not good news because wet weather will cause an insect explosion. 'Valuable food crops would be gobbled up by millions of insect pests.'[3]

The Globe science textbook *Concepts and Challenges in Earth Science* uses a similar device to indicate the catastrophe caused by global warming. This text shows a drawing of the New York City skyline with the water level higher than the Statue of Liberty and most buildings except the World Trade Center towers. The text includes the statement: 'In fact, if the ice caps of Antarctica and the Arctic melted, the sea level would rise 61m' (Bernstein, 1991).

World Resources Institute president Gus Speth tells readers:

'Global climate change is one of the gravest threats facing our planet. The buildup of carbon dioxide and other heat-trapping gases

---

[3] Special Introductory issue of *Science Gazette*, 'Kids Discover Weather,' Englewood, NJ: Prentice Hall.

in the atmosphere threatens to damage agricultural lands, forests and wildlife, and coastal regions.'

The primer, *50 Simple Things Kids Can do to Save the Earth*, tells children:

> 'Factories, electric power plants, and cars are making a lot of new gases...these new gases are trapping more and more of the sun's heat. This is called the greenhouse effect, or global warming... Every kid can help stop the greenhouse effect by using less energy, protecting and planting trees, and by recycling so factories don't need to work as hard making things' (Andrews and McMeel, in Javna (ed.), 1990, p. 15).

These excerpts are not the exception. Patti Sinclair, author of *E for Environment: An Annotated Bibliography of Children's Books with Environmental Themes*, says: 'The books are pessimistic, quickly dated, preachy, and don't reflect a variety of opinions. Nine out of ten books treat global warming as fact rather than theory' (*Environmental Almanac*, 1994, p. 24).

It seems that the truth loses out if a more sensational version is plausible. Typical lessons teach children that acid rain is destroying our forests; overpopulation will exhaust our resources; the ozone layer is rapidly being destroyed; and global warming will lead to disastrous climatic change. Yet, each of these, and many other scare scenarios, have been widely debated or refuted by experts.[4] Nonetheless, they are taught as facts, rather than hypotheses, to children.

These examples illustrate a further serious problem with environmental education as it is currently taught: it emphasises issues, rather than sequential teaching of natural processes.

Who Needs Science?

When asked to write about the environment, children overwhelmingly focus on apocalyptic issues: global warming, acid rain, ozone depletion, overpopulation, resource depletion, water pollution, species extinction, and so on. Rarely, if ever, do we read about a child's celebration of the wonders of nature. Yet, most

---

[4] See for example, Bailey *et al.* (1995), or Bast *et al.* (1994).

children can spend hours on their bellies examining an anthole or watching a preying mantis stalk an unsuspecting insect. Educational children's stores are filled with tools to help kids explore the wonders of nature – bug jars, flower presses, identification books, magnifying glasses, for example. Many children lose this sense of wonder and appreciation for nature soon after starting school, unless they have parents or other adults nearby who spend time with them in the outdoors.

Rather than taking advantage of children's innate curiosity and powers of observation, environmental education programmes often start right in with 'issues' teaching. Recycling is perhaps the most widespread environmental issue, perhaps because it is easy to prescribe specific actions – actions even a nursery pupil can master.

At a July 1995 conference for environmental educators[5], I attended a teacher's demonstration entitled 'Nature's For Me' which is geared towards the nursery pupil. By its title, I thought I might find a good example of solid naturalist teaching. Instead, the first exercise was a song to teach pre-schoolers, sung to the tune, 'So Early in the Morning'. It goes like this:

'This is the way we rinse the can, rinse the can, rinse the can. This is the way we rinse the can, for re-cy-cal-ling.

This is the way we smash the can, smash the can, smash the can. This is the way we smash the can, for re-cy-cal-ling.

This is the way we bundle the papers, bundle the papers, bundle the papers. This is the way we bundle the papers, for re-cy-cal-ling.'

In 1995, the City of Ann Arbor renewed a substantial grant to the local nonprofit Ecology Center of Ann Arbor to conduct both adult and children's environmental education programmes. The pre-school and kindergarten programme is called We Recycle. It too has a song:[6]

---

5 Sponsored by the Virginia Department of Environmental Quality in Arlington, VA, 10-11 August, 1995.

6 'We Recycle: A Pre-School/Kindergarten Program,' enclosure with letter dated 9 August 1995 to the Michigan Centre for Environmental Studies sent by Nancy Stone, Solid Waste Educational Services Co-ordinator, City of Ann Arbor, MI.

'If you recycle and you know it, clap your hands

If you recycle and you know it, then the world will surely show it,

If you recycle and you know it, clap your hands.'

The programme also preaches its message through a puppet show, featuring Nellie Newspaper, Gordon Glass, Polly Plastic, and Tina Tin. The stated concept is 'What can be recycled and how to prepare recyclables. And, don't throw things away.'

Patti Sinclair, who has reviewed over 2,000 environmental books for children, also noticed the emphasis on issues. She found that certain issues, regions, and habitats go completely ignored while others are repeatedly published. Her list of current driving issues includes rainforests, acid rain, global warming, and ozone depletion. Sinclair challenges us to find books on temperate African rainforests. 'You'll come up dry. Look for books on tropical South American rainforests and you'll be flooded.' Similarly, she found that acid rain books outnumber general ecology books (Environmental Almanac, 1994, p. 25). 'Many children are learning about disappearing rainforests before they know what a rainforest is,' says Ginny Moore Kruse, director of the Cooperative Children's Book Center at the University of Wisconsin and author of *Children's Books in Print, 1993*.

These comments, again, are not unusual. Jeffrey Salmon, executive director of the George C. Marshall Institute, has been interviewing school teachers for the institute's project on environmental education (Independent Commission on Environmental Literacy, April 1997). 'I'm tired of hearing about another school that created a rainforest in its halls.'

We can interpret this as showing how such teaching is socially and politically oriented, rather than scientifically based. Consider the following discussion about population issues.

'Already there is not enough food for everyone. To produce more, ancient forests and wilderness areas are cleared and turned into farmland, causing the people and wild creatures that lived there to lose their homes. The land is sprayed with chemical fertilizers, weed killers, and pesticides in an attempt to grow more and better crops. These chemicals sometimes poison the food and water supply' (Kerven, 1992, p. 5).

How many fallacies and half-truths can be found in this single paragraph? Authors Julian Simon (Simon, 1984), Steven Moore (Bailey (ed.), 1995), and Dennis T. Avery,[7] to name a few, would argue that nearly every concept in the paragraph is flawed. Totally absent is a factual analysis of resource abundance and scarcity or land use. Also absent is any discussion of trade-offs or basic economics.

A World without Trade-Offs

Perhaps one of the biggest pitfalls of the Eco-kid movement is its failure to teach children the tools for thinking – how to approach an issue, how to examine the alternatives, how to develop solutions. They are told explicitly what to do, not how to think. The emphasis is not on the physical sciences, such as learning about hydrologic systems or about the unique ecosystem of the estuary. Instead, kids are taught soundbites about wetlands and endangered species loss or acid rain destruction.

Worse yet, children are receiving an issues-based education without a vital understanding about policy – that it involves trade-offs. In order for kids to hold strong opinions about environmental issues, they need to understand the alternative choices and the advantages or disadvantages that each choice entails.

In discussions about how we must conserve energy, Vice-President Al Gore responds to 13-year-old Sarah Muller's query about fossil fuels. Gore says:

'We must make a concerted effort to reduce our dependence on fossil fuels, such as oil, that create a lot of pollution when we use them for energy. Instead, we need to be developing and using more alternative fuels, like clean-burning natural gas, and renewable energy sources such as hydroelectricity, solar power and wind power' (*Newsweek*, 29 March 1993, p. 17).

---

[7] See, for example, *Global Food Progress* (1991).

99

He misinforms by suggesting natural gas is not a fossil fuel. He further damages the education process by avoiding any consideration of trade-offs. What do we give up and what do we gain in switching from one energy source to another? Is it possible that certain regions of the country may find it beneficial to rely more on one type of energy source than another? Instead, alternatives are framed in morally or politically correct terms.

In *50 Simple Things Kids Can do to Save the Planet*, the failure to understand trade-offs is evident in a discussion about batteries. In it, rechargeable batteries are politically correct, throwaway ones are not. The author explains to children: 'When [rechargeable batteries] get run down, you put them into a little box called a recharger. The recharger plugs into an electrical outlet. Then it takes electricity from the outlet and puts it into the battery.' (Jaune, 1990, pp.106-07). There seems to be no need to discuss the relative advantages of each type of battery, or how the power gets to the 'little box'.

The failure to understand trade-offs explains how reasonable it really was for 11-year-old David Moser to write: 'I don't know why somebody made CFCs and halons, but I do think it was a dumb idea'(p. 19). Without thinking about trade-offs, we don't have to consider that food poisoning is at an all-time low where refrigeration is common, or that people are more comfortable, healthier, and productive in air-conditioned environments during hot, humid seasons.

Ironically, the only discussion I could find of trade-offs in *50 Simple Things* comes in a section which encourages kids to become junk food detectives. After talking about how entrepreneurs destroy rain forests in order to raise cattle to produce beef for fast-food outlets in the US, eco-kids are encouraged to stop eating at fast-food restaurants. Anticipating the uproar this might create, the author concedes 'What if we like fast food?' After telling kids to go to those that sell us the least rubbish, or that recycle, he ultimately conceded the existence of trade-offs:

'You see, it's not always easy to decide what to do. In order to save the Earth, we often have to make tough choices. But then...what other choice do we have if we really care?'(pp. 148-149).

The Kid's Earth Handbook rightly informs children that 'recycling paper costs more than making paper from new wood pulp'. Of course, it adds, 'but it saves trees'. Struggling with the problem of reconciling the politically-correct need to recycle with the sheer economics of recycling, the author concludes:

> 'Unfortunately, because recycled paper does take special facilities, it's more expensive. So only a small percentage of the paper purchased by the world's market is recycled paper. The United States could change this since it is the leading consumer of newsprint, using 40 percent of the world's supply' (Markle, 1991).

Children fail to learn that politically-correct choices have their costs. What might the children say if we instead asked them: 'If we choose to postpone the widespread use of recycled paper until it becomes more cost effective, how could we alternatively use the money we've saved to enhance the environment?'

Instead, environmentally-correct choices are viewed as right, and costless. As every attentive eco-kid knows, oil is bad, hydroelectric is good. Disposable nappies are bad, cloth nappies are good. Landfills are bad, recycling is good. Automobiles are bad, bikes are good. Using pine or oak wood is good, using rainforest woods is bad. Steven West wrote to his Congressmen about his concerns about the ozone layer: 'My suggestion is that we limit how many aerosol and gasoline products we buy ... or we could get scientists to invent a substitute for CFCs to put in the sprayers' (Schwartz, 1990, p. 158). Wow! Isn't that simple?

I've talked in terms of trade-offs to my 5-year-old daughters ever since they could listen. Even at their young age, they understand everyday trade-offs. If we buy that toy today, we use up money that can be used to purchase other things. The toy is not good or bad – it simply represents one way we can use our resources. Yet that perspective is a far cry from the litany of rights and wrongs in the environment. What are some of the teaching tools to teach these rights and wrongs? Besides the endless lists of 'do's and don'ts' consider this typical example: *Earth Book for Kids* urges kids to 'do something about garbage'. They are told to start an educational campaign to tell others about recycling centres. Create

101

a display to make people more aware of the 'acute landfill space shortage' and to encourage them to recycle (*ibid.,* p. 25).

While students may be adept at describing the evils of landfills, few can satisfactorily tell you exactly why something is classified as an environmental good or bad. Children are drilled to accept, for example, that recycling is the only proper way to deal with resources. By coercing their parents to sort paper, plastic, aluminum, and glass, and then to haul it all out to the curbside, the children are making their environmental mark on the world. With this clean conscience, there's no need to look at the facts. To name a few: each additional recycling truck rumbling through the neighbourhood adds vehicle emissions to the air, consumes oil and gas, and increases noise pollution. At the recycling plants, energy is consumed to process the materials, and huge volumes of waste water or other wastes are released to the environment. In other words, sometimes recycling is more environmentally friendly, sometimes it is not. It depends upon what we are trying to maximise or achieve. But this is not typically a topic of discussion. More likely, recycling is viewed as the end-all and the educational focus is finding ways to get others to recycle. In the words of the Alley Foundation's book, 'Cry out to others to cut down on their waste and to recycle whenever possible!' (The Alley Foundation, 1991).

Values Teaching Back in the Classroom

Amidst discussions about the loss of traditional values teaching in the classroom, values teaching is alive and well, at least in the realm of environmental education. In *Defining Environmental Education,* a project funded by the US Environmental Protection Agency (EPA), authors John Disinger and Martha C. Monroe explain how environmental education differs from environmental science: 'environmental education is concerned with values and skills as well as knowledge.' Differing personal values, they write, 'make it difficult to derive the facts' (Disinger and Monroe). What more dangerous a statement can one find regarding threats to the integrity of education?

Given this values approach, it's not surprising to see, for example, some of the programmes in the Ann Arbor, MI, curriculum. '50 Ways to Look at a Paper Cup' asks young kids to 'Take a commonly disposed of item like a paper cup, plastic fork or an action figure toy and brainstorm questions about it. Here are some questions to start you off: Where did it come from? How could it be reused? *What does it say about the people who use it?*'[8] The school programme, incidentally, is sponsored by the Ecology Centre of Ann Arbor and funded by the City of Ann Arbor and the Michigan Department of Natural Resources. It should raise a red flag about the value of bringing outside special interests into the classrooms.

Disinger and Monroe perhaps clarify the value of these programmes by their broader description of environmental education:

> '...environmental education is not just a topic; its goals include more than learning information. *EE is driven by a mission*: to produce a concerned citizenry that is intellectually and psychologically prepared to confront and resolve environmental issues.'

They further explain: '...the environmental education community's identification of skills and values related to behavior change as an integral component of environmental literacy puts it at odds with traditional educational practice' (Disinger and Monroe, undated). This, an article defining environmental education, shares my concern about environmental education's diversion from education. Yet, our conclusions are diametrically opposed. While I argue for a return to traditional, science-based teaching, environmentalists see a need for greater strategies to modify behaviour. In other words, they want to enhance their ability to turn out advocates.

In order to understand and effect 'the full range of motives available for behavior change,' Disinger and Monroe recognise the following framework for environmental education: first, Ecological

---

8   The Recycling and Education Station Program, Ecology Centre of Ann Arbor, MI and
     the MI Department of Natural Resources.

Concepts, second, Conceptual Awareness, third, Issues Investigation and Evaluation, and fourth, Environmental Action Skills ('It is clear that more emphasis needs to be placed on the ...third and fourth ones.') In addition, environmental behaviours can be 'enhanced' by teaching social marketing techniques and altering the programme service dimensions.

> 'These principles include understanding the full range of motives available for behavior change, removing real and perceived barriers to change, providing procedural information, establishing social commitment, highlighting the actions of opinion leaders and role models, and avoiding approaches that can trigger unwanted actions.'

Non-conformists are Evil

With an emphasis on the environmentally-correct and behaviour modification, one interesting feature of environmentalist-based teaching is its targeting of non-conformists. The underlying message is that those who do not adhere to an acceptable vision of the Earth clearly prefer a foul environment over a pristine one.

Hooker Chemical Move Over... Here Come the Lumberjacks

A decade or so ago, 'big industry' represented the clearest symbol of evil to the environmentalists. But today, some designated 'bad guys' might surprise even an avowed nature lover. During the 1980s, I remember a conversation in which a friend reluctantly shared her father's source of employment. With downcast eyes, she quietly explained that he worked for Hooker Chemical, the fall guy for the Love Canal incident in upper New York State. When toxic chemicals were found oozing into the basements of several houses in the neighbourhoods, the blame was placed on Hooker Chemical. Clearly, she had become accustomed to bearing the blame for the events at Love Canal. But today, kids do not know of Hooker Chemical. They do not need to. They have lumberjacks.

The president of the Mountain States Legal Foundation, Perry Pendley, addressed an association of lumbermen in Des Moines, Iowa. One of the participants described the antagonism he felt when he visited his son's fourth grade class to talk about his profession. The students were hostile towards him for being a logger. Another showed an exercise his pre-school child brought home. The kids were asked to pick the picture that 'did not belong'. The first three pictures showed three animals in the woods – a deer, a fox, and a squirrel. The fourth? A logger. Which one does not belong?

Writing for the *Washington Post*, Bob Garfield humorously shared his surprise at seeing the third entry on his 9-year-old's homework assignment of 'Pet peeves'. Just after prejudice and murder, his daughter's biggest peeve is lumberjacks. Reminding readers that his suburban daughter has likely never met a lumberjack, he describes how the environmental education curriculum equates cutting down trees as the moral equivalent of genocide (Garfield, 1994).

Rita Carlson, a specialist in natural resources and public lands with Alliance for America, shares the following story: In a small town in northern Washington State, teachers gave a class of second graders a test on dinosaurs. The first three asked questions about the behaviour and traits of the dinosaurs: where they lived, which ones ate meat, and how they caught food. The fourth question, quite tenuously linked to dinosaurs, asked 'which way do people endanger animals?' Children were to circle the picture that best answered the question. The choices were A) a man patting a dog, B) a girl stroking a cat, C) a forest with a skidder setting by a deck of logs and a logging truck, and D) a corral full of horses (Carlson, 1995).

How is the environmental education system fostering these anti-lumberjack attitudes? Consider one comment in a chapter called 'The Politics of a Cleaner Planet' in *The Kids' Environment Book: What's Awry and Why*. Author Anne Pederson writes:

'There are always those who, when faced with the prospect of change, say that nothing is wrong and things should remain just the way they are....many people lose sight of the greater good and focus just on what's going to happen to them. For instance, in spring 1990, the northern spotted owl was declared a threatened species. This means a reduction of the heavy logging in the Pacific Northwest forests where the owl lives. This is a responsible decision from an environmental point of view. One, it saves a species. Two, it saves trees from being cut down; most of that lumber is being sent to Japan, anyway' (Pederson, 1991, pp. 149-150).

Aside from the targeted anti-timbermen attitude, children are taught to be suspicious of anyone who does not buy into the environmentally-correct vision. In *Earth Book for Kids*, children are encouraged to survey relatives, neighbours, and classmates about their recycling habits. The first two questions ask if they recycle and why. The third question asks: 'If you do not make a conscious effort to reuse and/or recycle, which ones of these statements reflect reasons you do not? a) I really haven't given it much thought, b) I don't have enough space to collect recyclables, c) I don't know where the nearest recycling center is, d) It's too much trouble, e) I know the environment is in trouble, but I really don't care' (Schwartz, 1990, p. 19).

Clearly missing is the response f) 'I do recycle by re-using materials where practical, but I do not participate in organized recycling programs because I believe they consume more resources than they conserve.' But the advocate's perspective is that you simply do not care.

The EarthWorks Group has an explanation for kids about these people who don't care.

'It helps that many people now know about the dangers of pollution and the benefits of doing things like recycling and saving energy. But other people seem not to know – or not to care. People who seem not to care are almost never *bad people* – they are just scared to get involved. They are afraid of being criticized for taking the lead or for doing something "different". Or maybe they are just a little lazy. Let's face it, it *is* easier to just hang out or watch television than to clean up a beach or write a letter to your senator!' (Dee, 1991, p. 7).

Write a Letter to your Senator!

The EarthWorks Group raises another central feature of environmental education. Despite criticisms about the lack of science education, the lack of decision-making teaching, and the preponderance of misinformation and hype, children are encouraged to take assigned advocacy positions and become politically active.

Nearly every environmentalist book aimed at children devotes entire sections to activism. A sampling of headings includes: 'More ways to make every day Earth day', 'Where to write', 'Getting to Work', and 'How you can Help'.

50 Simple Things urges kids to write to their US Senators, write to the President, write to world leaders (it includes the addresses for Gorbachev and Japan's Prime Minister Kaifu). Or, join an environmental group. Those listed, not surprisingly, include the Natural Resources Defense Council, famous for its alar apple scam;[9] and Greenpeace, the group that paid hunters to skin baby seals alive for a film, simply to give the impression that this is traditional hunting practice. (It is not, by the way, a standard practice.)

On the Internet, the Rainforest Action Network Information Service provides a list of resources for teachers and students. Entries include 'The Kid's Guide to Social Action,' and 'Global Response – Young Environmentalist's Action Newsletter' – 'an environmental action network dedicated to letter writing focusing attention on specific planetary environmental threats.'

Recommended books for kids in Friends of the Earth's *Environmental Education Resource Guide* include *Going Green: A Kid's Handbook to Saving the Planet, 50 Simple Things Kids Can Do to Save the Earth,* and *Earth Book for Kids: Activities to Help Heal the Earth.* Newsweek's *Just for Kids!?!* publication recommends *Save our Planet: 750 Everyday Ways You Can Help Clean Up the Earth.*

The textbook, *Your Health*, published by Prentice-Hall, also encourages children to 'Consider joining an environment group'. Its suggestions for further contacts include Greenpeace, Zero Population Growth, Planned Parenthood, and Earth First! (a group that has solicited terminally-ill people to undertake life-threatening

---

9 See for example, Kwong Echard (1990), pp. 31-40.

eco-terrorist activities). And *Kid Heroes of the Environment*, another publication of The Earth Works Group, praises children for conducting petition drives, organising letter writing campaigns to political leaders, and boycotting businesses. Nearly every one of the 'Kid Heroes' was focused on changing someone else's behaviour. (An outstanding exception, by the way, is the true kid hero, Christian Miller. Concerned about the loss of sea turtle habitat, Christian cleaned up a beach area and, on a daily basis, monitors and protects turtle nests, eggs, and hatchlings. He further keeps a data base, adding valuable information about the sea turtles' numbers.) (Dee, 1991, pp. 18-19.)

From Hollywood, The (Kirsty) Alley Foundation, 'a non-political, non-profit organization dedicated to the environmental education of our youth', distributes a book called 'Cry Out' which is dedicated to 'those who understand that the time to save the Earth is now'. It tells the children:

> 'Unless you take action NOW, the beautiful forests where you go hiking, the beaches where you swim in clean water, the clear morning when you take a breath of sweet-smelling air could all become things of the past. This booklet will give you an idea of some of the many things you can do.'

For the most part, we are not giving children sufficient information to foster meaningful activism. Armed with knowledge and problem solving, children can select and develop their own projects and activities. Instead, prescribed letter writing campaigns are immensely popular with teachers.

Environmental policy analyst Jonathan Adler had the opportunity to review letters written by classrooms of schoolchildren who wrote to the Food and Drug Administration about bioengineered produce. 'Their letters didn't address the scientific or even, really, the ethical issues: They were about death! They called the biotech tomato "Franken Tomato", and they pleaded, "Please don't do this, I don't want to die!" 'The letters were written all at once and they were similar,' continues Adler. 'I'd call that brainwashing' (Poore, 1993, p. 30).

Children need scientific knowledge to understand environmental issues. This includes studies of botany, ecology, hydrology, entomology, and so on. They also need to understand the basic scientific method: that scientific hypotheses need to be corroborated with observation and experimentation. Of course, some of this is technically beyond the understanding of the younger ones, but if they aren't able to understand the science, they also shouldn't be called upon to lobby for specific policy options.

Burdening our Kids

'One of the reasons that the environmental situation is as bad as it is is because of people's attitudes. For years men and women have exploited the world's resources without much thought about where that exploitation might be taking them...And when a problem arises, no one wants to take responsibility for it. People either shrug it off or pretend that it doesn't exist.

OK, so you're a kid. But you'll be an adult sooner than you think. If we continue living the way we do now, how much ozone will there be in the stratosphere to protect you ten years from now? How much drinkable water underground? Will the place where you live be too hot for comfort then? Will the air be fit to breathe?' (Pederson, 1991, p. 155).

Is it possible that we are taking our adult perceptions and concerns and placing the burden squarely on the shoulders of kids? As we bemoan the fact that kids are growing up before their time, in light of drugs, alcohol, violence, and other social problems, isn't it time the environmental educators reconsidered their strategies? On the most basic level, we are taking the fun out of being a kid. By teaching issues from the time children enter nursery, we are destroying the very characteristics of children that we all admire and relish – their ability to find sheer joy in the simplest things.

What are the things that children cherish? Crayons, crafts, toys, balloons – all things that have been linked with evil in children's environmentalism. Here are some excerpts from the runaway bestseller, *50 Simple Things Kids Can do to Save the Earth.*

'Helium balloons? Big, bouncing, bobbing...Oops? When helium balloons are released, they are often blown by strong winds into the ocean. Even if the sea is hundreds of miles away, balloons can still land there. Sometimes sea creatures think balloons are food and eat them. Sea turtles, for example, eat jellyfish – which look and wiggle just like clear balloons. If a turtle makes a mistake and eats a balloon, the balloon can block its stomach. So the turtle can starve to death. Whales sometimes accidentally swallow balloons that are floating in the ocean. The balloons get stuck inside the whale's stomach, and can kill the creature!' (Andrews and McMeel, 1990, p. 73).

Similarly, it tells children, 'most crayons are made from oil. Since oil comes from prehistoric creatures, you might be coloring with the last remains of a Tyrannosaurus Rex!' (*ibid.,* p. 32). Or 'Have you ever made pictures with markers? Some have chemicals with names like "toluene and ethanol" in them. Creating these chemicals makes pollution and uses oil. Glue Sticks, rubber cement and glue sometimes have the same types of pollution-causing chemicals in them.'

Even toys do not escape the wrath of environmental education. 'Toys just don't come from toy stores. They come from materials taken out of the Earth. So if they break right away, and you have to buy new ones to replace them, you're not only creating a lot of extra garbage, you're using up the treasures of the Earth' (*ibid.,* p. 24).

Stuffed animals are also not spared in the quest to create eco-warriors. One parent told how his child's teacher asked the children to bring in their favourite stuffed animal. As the children sat in a circle, cuddling their beloved friends, the teacher told them how the real-life counterparts to these animals are being pushed to extinction as a result of man's greedy behaviour.

More recently, children's trainers have come under attack. Trainers that sport the red lights in the heels are immensely popular with kids. But, the movement teaches that mercury from the batteries either pollutes the groundwater when it leaches out of landfills or pollutes the air when it is incinerated. Even though most of today's landfills carefully guard against leaching, and the amount of mercury from the small batteries is minuscule in comparison to other real hazards, activist campaigns have been 'successful'. One manufacturer offers a toll free number that kids can call. They will receive a mailing package to return their shoes to the manufacturer who will then 'properly dispose' of the offending item. Never mind that the kids are now out a pair of trainers – they have, however, assuaged somebody's environmental guilt.

3. The Corruption of Environmental Education

The problems with environmental education stem largely from its emphasis on *environmentalism*, rather than *education*. Until we embrace the educational aspects, we will fail to achieve environmental literacy. How have we ended up with the misguided advocacy approach that now dominates educational programmes?

Michael Weilbacher, president of Pennsylvania Association for Environmental Education, is concerned about the piecemeal model of environmental education, rather than a sequential curriculum of naturalist and environmental education:

> 'For so many years, mainstream educators wouldn't let environmental education in the front door. So they entered through any door they could, attaching themselves to programs where ever they could. We built our environmental education curriculum like we build Frankenstein: we keep gluing body parts together. As a result, we have no focused instruction that is sequenced from beginning to end.'

The piecemeal approach has been perpetuated by the tendency of teachers to invite outside 'experts' to address the classroom. Often environmental groups, local parks, and other non-profit organisations offer their services to teachers. Weilbacher warns against accepting these offers:

> 'Keep in mind that these positions are typically staffed by young, inexperienced people. The turnover rate at these organizations is high. In most cases, the regular classroom teacher knows more than the so-called expert. These outsiders should not be the teachers.'

In other instances, the teachers themselves are not sufficiently educated to teach the materials they attempt. Consider that the United Nations Environment Programme markets its publication, *Environmental Education for Our Common Future*, to teachers *'whatever subject they teach' (Unesco Courier*, December 1992, p.

25). Without proper training, environmental education can resort to slogans teaching and endless lists of do's and don'ts – lists widely featured in nearly every environmental education book.

The growth of environmental education, particularly its reliance on and infusion of environmental advocates, has also been supported by the state and federal governments. In 1990, President Bush signed the National Environmental Education Act, appropriating $65 million over five years to set up an Office of Environmental Education within the EPA. The office serves as a clearinghouse for green educational materials. One of the goals of EPA's Environmental Education Division is to educate and motivate youth by: increasing the number of teachers that 'infuse environmental education into existing curricula', and providing educators with access to quality environmental education materials (US Environmental Protection Agency, October 1993, p. 6).

The Environmental Education Division's (EED) agenda emphasises 'the creation of links with existing networks of environmental educators, environmentalists, and students'. Its support for environmental special interest groups is clear:

> 'Environmental groups have the qualifications and experience to be of considerable assistance to EED in establishing innovative and effective educational programs and activities. EED will work closely with all interested environmental organizations to ensure that the office stays on the cutting edge of environmental trends' (*ibid.*, p. 4).

The problem, of course, is the focus on trends. As we devote vast resources to trends teaching, we need to look down the road and wonder if it will prove useful when new trends arise.

Beyond the federal level, at least 30 states have formal programmes of environmental education, each with fairly similar missions of creating specific environmental characteristics within its citizenry. The State of Wyoming recognises

> 'that it has a great opportunity to advance environmental education. ...The experience that will create environmentally literate and responsible citizens can and should be woven into the fabric of our schools. For example, the study of solid waste disposal in science could be paralleled with studies in language arts classes. Students

113

could write creatively about the problem, using strategies such as essays, poems or letters. Environmental problems and solutions lend themselves to the integration of subjects. Integration and relevancy are two terms that must be of central importance to the restructuring of schools' (Wyoming Department of Education, 1994).

While this may sound like a great idea, consider the bias that is introduced in an assignment of precisely this nature in a National Geographic Society teacher's guide. In its curriculum for science and language arts, National Geographic suggests this activity: 'Have the children write or dictate stories about two imaginary planets, "Trashoid 4" and "Recyclet". What would the planets look like? How would they be different? What would the beings who live on these planets look like? How would they live?' (National Geographic Society, 1992). In a related exercise, children are given the assignment 'A World of Difference', and asked to draw a picture of 'what you think the Earth could look like someday if we let trash pile up,' and 'Now turn your paper over and draw a picture of what the Earth could look like if we all recycle.' It's not over yet! Lastly, 'Colour your pictures, then save this paper to wrap a small gift.' The toted skills reviewed include: 'creative expression, applying information, and reinforcing concepts.'

Yet, hope is on the horizon. In the State of Virginia, the Department of Education has recently made a commitment to a strong science-based programme. James Firebaugh, Science Specialist for the department, believes 'scientific literacy and environmental literacy go hand in hand'. Since the spring of 1994, the department has been redefining and redirecting its standards of learning. The 1995 standards emphasise knowledge and comprehension through investigation (the scientific method) and understanding (knowledge application). One of the overriding goals of the revisions has been to delay the introduction of complex issues too early in the teaching sequence. Cautioning that the programme is not about advocacy, but rather sound science, the first issues analysis is introduced in the fifth grade or later.

In Arizona, there is also a move afoot to return to a science-based education. In 1990, the state adopted an environmental education law to promote knowledge of the environment, develop positive attitudes and encourage social responsibility toward environmental issues. When the law came up for re-authorisation in the spring of 1994, a committee was established to rewrite the guidelines. 'There was a growing concern that environmental education is more of a propagandizing exercise in some cases than an educational exercise,' said the state Senate Majority Leader Tom Patterson (Noyes, 1994). Professor Michael Sanera, who has written a parents' primer about the dangers of environmental education (Sanera and Shaw, 1996), has prepared a set of new guidelines which include:

- Students will understand that scientists do not always agree on the 'facts';

- Many environmental issues involve economic trade-offs;

- Government actions to protect the environment have intended and unintended consequences; and

- Increases in economic wealth lead to protection of the environment and healthier populations.

'Arizona is the only state so far to reform its environmental education law striking out behavioral modification and requiring all environmental education be based on economics and sound science,' says Professor Sanera.[1]

---

[1] Personal interview with Professor Sanera, 17 August 1995.

4. Towards a Curriculum for Achieving Environmental Literacy

An excellent basis for a revised environmental education model has been developed by Michael Weilbacher, president of Pennsylvania Association for Environmental Education. I supplement his model in a couple of ways to arrive at the following seven components:

1. Nature Study

Foremost, children need to spend more time outdoors. Young children, especially, are fascinated with bugs, birds, and trees! My girls are keen on identifying the birds that come to our birdfeeders. The hummingbird feeder, bird nest boxes, and simple bird baths give the kids a good sense of the habitat needs of different species. 'We have to rescue nature study from the 1950s, along with outdoor education. When you graduate from the 12th grade, you should know the plants and animals in your neighborhood,' prescribes Weilbacher. Moreover, children have to understand the little issues before they can tackle the big ones. If the climate is changing, as environmental advocates claim, then the plants and animals that live in our backyards will start changing. But if we do not know what lives there, we cannot possibly notice. We need to apply our understanding of local issues to broader problems.

2. Conservation

Along with nature study, we need to resurrect the study of conservation. Conservation, the study of the wise use of natural and environmental resources, has been opposed by many environmental advocates who instead, seek to preserve natural resources by prohibiting their use. Yet, it is simply irrational to overlook the fact that we need to use resources to live on the Earth. Our best move is to learn to use resources wisely, with an eye towards long-range sustainability and the health of the planet.

3. Core Sciences

'Environmental education,' says Weilbacher, 'spent too much time trying to disassociate itself from science, claiming that it is a special process. But, if environmental education is anything, it is understanding how the world operates and that is science.'

At a time when educators seek ways to boost science scores, it seems obvious that environmental science can be the vital link. Introduce outdoor education early in the teaching process, and continue with natural and physical sciences.

4. Issues

Those who can distance themselves from advocacy agree on one thing: issues teaching needs to be postponed until children have a good information and problem solving basis. Virginia's Department of Education specialist, James Firebaugh, recommends issues teaching begins no earlier than the 5th grade. Weilbacher also agrees that issues need to come later in the teaching sequence. Children should know where Brazil is, for example, before they talk about rainforests. 'I'm just not big on making 6- and 7-year olds worry about global dilemmas. Adults might feel a sense of urgency in their perceptions of environmental problems, but that's the adult's problem. If they feel a problem is so urgent, they should take action themselves, rather than using the kids.'

5. Action

The current environmental education model clearly fosters action. But, in many cases, the actions are the result of a teacher's one-sided approach to the issue (Disinger and Monroe). And more often than not, the actions, as case studied in the book, *Kid Heroes of the Environment*, entail pressuring other people to undertake prescribed environmental advocacy actions.

The best actions are those that children design, develop, and undertake themselves, based on broad-based knowledge about the problem and its impacts. The aforementioned instance of Christian Miller's project to save sea turtles is an excellent example of environmental action based on knowledge, analysis, and true concern. 'Abandon litter programs along with the slogans. It's a nice civic action, but not adding to environmental literacy. Let the kids decide ... if they've gone through a solid program of literacy, they will pick good projects,' says Weilbacher.

6. Advocacy

Here, I offer a divergence from Weilbacher. I view advocacy along the lines of high school debate. 'Advocacy' can be used as an exercise to hone problem-solving skills, argumentation, and public speaking skills. Rather than promoting behavioural modification skills, as Disinger and Monroe have proposed, I see advocacy as an applied communication skill. It is important that children learn to formulate their own opinions and present reasoned analysis to justify their beliefs. In the spirit of diverse values, we should teach that it is acceptable for others to have differing values and opinions. The key is for kids to have a firm foundation for establishing their own positions. Coercing others to agree should be outside the realm of education.

7. Economics

Here again, I am adding my own perspective to the Weilbacher model. I believe children need to integrate both science and economics to understand public policy. Issues teaching without trade-offs and alternatives gives rise to fantasy problem solving. I'm not advocating the teaching of micro- and macro-economics to children, but rather the basic concepts of choices in actions. When we choose one action, others are precluded. When we devote money to pursue one project, others are not funded. When we select Plan A, it is likely to have consequences upon B, C, and D.

The integration of these skills can provide students with a sound overall education: one that will enable them to apply their reasoning to a wide range of problems, not just those that are currently trendy with environmentalists. It will foster a confidence in decision-making and an ability to see alternative options. These skills are useful, regardless of the children's future vocations and professions. Clearly absent from the proposed model is the current environmental education emphasis on behaviour modification. In a nation where we have deviated from most reasonable notions of individual responsibility, environmental education can help guide us back to a focus on our own abilities and contributions.

5. Conclusions – And A Word From Your Sponsors

As an endnote, let me share some of the other sources of 'environmental education' that I came across during the course of this research. Beyond the traditional information sources, children are bombarded with environmentalism in virtually everything they come in contact with. Consider a few examples that may be surprising to those without young children. Endangered animals, in particular, are a theme which marketers have embraced with full force.

Food Packaging

Barnum's Animals Endangered Collection Crackers by Nabisco replaces the traditional animal cracker collection. Gone is the familiar circus animal theme, replaced with a lush green jungle scene. Kids can 'help save endangered animals around the world' every time they buy the collection – Nabisco is donating up to $100, 000 to the World Wildlife Fund from the cookie sales.

In the organic food stores, you can purchase Small World Animal Grahams and 'help save the animals'. On the back of the box, children read: 'Eat these cookies and help save endangered animals! Think of any wild animal. Chances are it's in trouble. That's because people have been hunting animals, polluting the land and oceans where they live, and destroying their homes to build houses and roads.'

If you buy a box of Annie's Totally Natural Macaroni & Cheese, you can send for a free 'Be Green' bumper sticker. Annie informs the kids: 'if a politician or corporate executive sees your "Be Green" bumper sticker, they may think twice about trashing the Planet...If you believe that a person will see your "Be Green" and be encouraged to help the Earth live, then *You* will have helped the Earth live. Thank you!'

Purina, the animal food manufacturer, advertises that 'Your little cats can help save endangered Big Cats'. Consumer purchases of

Purina cat products help bolster Purina's Big Cat Survival Fund which supports efforts to preserve endangered 'Big Cats'.

Fast food companies are particularly sensitive to creating a green image, so their propagandizing is not surprising. Burger King offers 'New Earth Happy Packaging', which tells kids 'You'll probably notice that our sandwiches now come served in paper wrapping instead of a box. That's because we figure the world could probably use 15,000 less tons of trash a year. And less trash means less trucks to carry it. Which means less gas and a lot less air pollution. Not to mention the reduction in packaging the packaging has to be shipped in!'

McDonald's trayliners provide an entire discourse on 'the many ways McDonald's Earth Effort is working to protect our environment'. It tells of 'McRecycle USA, Trash Reduction, Our Rain Forest Policy ("Tropical rain forests play a vital role in the Earth's ecology..."), Energy and Water Conservation, More Efforts for Our Earth, and We're Your Neighbors'.

Toys

Endangered species themes are also prevalent in children's games, puzzles, and other toys. The 'Endangered Animals Floor Puzzle' by Frank Schaeffer Publications, for example, received the Oppenheim Toy Portfolio 'best toy' award. Similarly, 'The Rain Forest Giant Floor Puzzle', also produced by Frank Schaeffer Publications, received the 1993 Parents' Choice Award from the Parents' Choice Foundation.

Another prevalent message amongst the popular culture of eco-kids focuses on the evil businessman. Consider the evolution of the GI Joe soldier doll. GI Joe now includes an 'Eco Warriors' series. One doll in the series goes by the code name CEO Cesspool. The CEO stands for Chief Environmental Operative. 'Cesspool was the Chief Executive Officer of a huge multi-national corporation with vast holdings in oil refineries, chemical plants and mills. In an effort to placate environmental groups that were constantly assailing him about the toxic wastes spewing from his operations, he took them on a tour through one of his chemical plants to prove his operations were environmentally sound. While demonstrating

120

the efficiency of a toxic waste containment area outside the plant, the scaffolding collapsed and he fell into the sludge below. The accident left him horribly disfigured.' Armed with an acid-assisting chainsaw, Cesspool hijacked a GI Joe supply train and added aerosol spray cans which contain CFCs to the monthly supplies. These cans pollute the environment and destroy the ozone layer. 'In the interest of keeping civilians informed, the enlisted personnel are encouraged to tell their friends and family the importance of protecting the environment.' Other eco-warriors in the series include Clean-sweep, Ozone, Sludge viper, and Toxo-viper.

Cartoons

I first started researching environmental education issues after seeing several episodes of Captain Planet, a popular save-the-Earth cartoon, courtesy of Ted Turner Broadcasting. The anti-human, anti-business, anti-science themes were all too obvious. Earlier this year, the Center for Media and Public Affairs in Washington, DC, reviewed children's cartoons and published its findings in *Doomsday Kids: Environmental Messages on Children's Television.*

'We found that when cartoons take on environmental issues, they frequently portray a world menaced by impending catastrophe...Over nine out of ten environmental plotlines evoke images of gloom and doom, such as mass extinction or environmental apocalypse... A majority of business characters are bad guys... Mad scientists play villains often enough to give scientists an even worse image than businessmen' (Lichter *et al.*, April 1995).

Music

The April 1995 issue of BMG Music Service's monthly catalogue, featured *Earth Day 25: Artists and music in Celebration of the 25th Anniversary of Earth Day.* With the claim that 'Nowhere ... has Earth Day been more championed and supported than in the music and entertainment industries', the catalogue of records, compact discs, and tapes offers environmental words of wisdom amongst the record advertisements. 'Inside these pages, you'll find sections on saving the rainforests, Earth Day benefit concerns, music inspired by nature, kid's stuff and more. We've even included helpful eco-tips and the addresses and telephone numbers of various environmental organisations like Greenpeace and The World Wildlife Fund.' Clearly, you can 'show that you care about the environment' by purchasing their 'great albums'.

These examples serve a vital purpose: we need to concern ourselves with the proper teaching of environmental science and policy. If we are to achieve environmental literacy, we cannot relegate teaching to the backs of cereal boxes, the Saturday morning cartoons, nor to environmental advocates in the classrooms.

Parting Remarks

The study of natural and environmental resources can invoke sheer fascination. But we have tended to elevate the study of the environment to apocalyptic scenarios of doom and gloom. By allowing environmental advocates to serve as educators, we have stifled the natural inclination of children to understand and probe the natural process. We need to distinguish between advocacy and education, and emphasise the latter if we want to achieve environmental literacy.

Our educational goal should not rest on lofty statements about behaviour modification. They should not foist a range of trendy slogans upon our kids. Should we choose to take advantage of their ability to mimic, let's teach them the names of the birds, butterflies, insects, trees, and other creatures in their own back yards. We can then enlarge their horizons as their knowledge base expands.

Our goals should be to open their eyes and to impart knowledge. Armed with knowledge, they can develop a world view in which science, technology, progress, and individual responsibility can foster a sound and healthy environment. That is true environmental literacy.

References

Alley Foundation (1991): *Cry Out: An Illustrated Guide to What you can do to Save the Earth*, Beverly Hills, CA: Galaxy Productions Inc.

Avery, D.T. (1991): *Global Food Progress 1991*, Indianapolis, IN: Hudson Institute.

Bailey, R. (ed.) (1995): *The True State of the Planet*, New York: The Free Press.

Bast, J., P.J. Hill, and R.C. Rue (1994): *Eco-Sanity*, Maryland: Madison Books.

Bernstein, L. (1991): *Concepts and Challenges in Earth Science*, Englewood Cliffs, NJ: Globe Book Co.

Bowker, R.R. (ed.) (1993): *Children's Books in Print 1993*, New Providence, NJ: R.R. Bowker Publishers.

Carlson, Rita (1995): 'What are they doing in our Schools?', *Alliance News*, Vol. 4, Issue 3, April/May.

Dee, C. (ed.) (1991): *Kid Heroes of the Environment*, Berkeley, CA: EarthWorks Press.

Disinger, J.F., and M.C. Monroe (undated): 'Defining Environmental Education', *The Environmental Education Toolbox Workshop Resource Manual*, Ann Arbor, MI: NCEET Publications.

Garfield, B. (1994): 'Little Chop of Horrors', *The Washington Post*, 1 May.

Hicks, S.R. (1991): 'Global Problems are Too Big for Little Kids', *Wall Street Journal*, 16 April.

Holt, T.H. (1991): 'Growing up Green', *Reason*, October.

Javna, J. (ed.) (1990): *50 Simple Things Kids Can Do to Save the Earth*, New York: Andrews and McMeel and The EarthWorks Group.

Kerven, R. (1992): *Saving Planet Earth*, New York: Franklin Watts.

Kwong Echard, J. (1990): *Protecting the Environment: Old Rhetoric, New Imperatives*, Washington, DC: Capital Research Center.

Lichter, R.S. *et al.* (1995): *Doomsday Kids: Environmental Messages on Children's Television*, Washington, DC: Center for Media and Public Affairs.

Markle, S. (1991): *The Kids' Earth Handbook*, Atheneium, New York: Maxwell Macmillan International.

Miles, B. (1991): *Save the Earth: An Action Handbook for Kids*, New York: Alfred A. Knopf.

Noyes, F. (1994): 'GOP Lawmakers Target Education on Environment', *The Arizona Daily Star*, 11 December.

Pederson, A. (1991): *The Kids' Environment Books: What's Awry and Why*, Santa Fe, NM: John Muir Publications.

Poore, P. (1993): 'Enviro Education: Is it Science, Civics – or Propaganda?', *Garbage*, April-May.

Sanera, M. and J.S. Shaw (1996): *Facts Not Fear: A Parent's Guide to Teaching Children About the Environment*, Washington, DC: Regnery Publishing.

Schwartz, L. (1990): *Earth Book for Kids: Activities to Help Heal the Environment*, Santa Barbara, CA: The Learning Works.

Simon, J. (1984): *The Resourceful Earth*, New York: Basil Blackwell Inc.

Sinclair, P.K. (1992): *E for Environment: An Annotated Bibliography of Children's Books with Environmental Themes*, New Providence, NJ: R.R. Bowker Publishers.

Snyder, R.E. *et al.* (1991): *Earth Science. The Challenge of Discovery*, ATE, Lexington, MA: D.C. Heath and Co.

Stone, N. (1995): 'Wee Recycle: A Pre-School/Kindergarten Program', enclosure and letter sent 9 August to Michigan Center for Environmental Studies.

Wallbank, W.T. (1993): *History and Life*, Glenview, IL: Scott Foresman.

Weilbacher, M. (1995): 'Fostering Personal Responsibility and Stewardship: The Role of Educators', presentation at the Conference for Environmental Educators, 10 August, Arlington, VA: Virginia Department of Environmental Quality.

Zuesse, E. (1981): 'Love Canal: The Truth Seeps Out', *Reason*, February, pp. 18-33.

(1997): 'Are We Building Environmental Literacy?', a report by the Independent Commission on Environmental Education, Washington, DC: George C. Marshall Institute.

(1992): 'Wonders of Learning Kit – Primary Level', Washington, DC: National Geographic Society.

(1992): 'Environmental Education for our Common Future', *The Unesco Courier*, December.

(1993): 'Saving the Earth', *Newsweek Just for Kids!?!*, 29 March.

(1993): 'KIDFORUM', KIDLINK computer network, <http:/www.kidlink.org>.

(1993): *Environmental Education – Outlook for the Future*, Washington, DC: United States Environmental Protection Agency, October.

(1993): 'Eco-Stories, Eco-Despair', *The 1994 Information Please Environmental Almanac*, Washington, DC: World Resources Institute.

(1994): 'Issue: Environment', *Culpeper Star-Exponent*, 26 February.

(1995): 'Earth Day Photo & Essay Contest Winners', *Delaware Coast Press*, 12 April.

(1994): 'Kids Discover Weather', special introductory issue of *Science Gazette*, Englewood, NJ: Prentice Hall.

IEA Education and Training Unit

The Education and Training Unit was established at the end of 1995, making it the youngest of the IEA's specialist units. The Unit aims to explore the part which markets can play in meeting the educational needs of individuals, families, communities and industry, hence reducing the role of the state.

Through its series of publications, and through conferences and seminars, the Unit seeks to promote public awareness of the theoretical underpinnings, current practice, and future potential, of education and training without the state.

The Institute of Economic Affairs

2 Lord North Street,
Westminster,
London SW1P 3LB
Tel: 0171 799 3745
Fax: 0171 799 2137
Email: iea@iea.org.uk
Internet:http://www.iea.org.uk

Independence

The Education and Training Unit is part of the Institute of Economic Affairs, a registered educational charity (No. 235351) founded in 1955. Like the IEA, the Education and Training Unit is financed from a variety of private sources to avoid over-reliance on any single or small group of donors.

All IEA publications are independently refereed and referees' comments are passed on anonymously to authors. The IEA gratefully acknowledges the contributions made to its educational work by the eminent scholars who act as its referees.

All the Institute's publications seek to further its objective of promoting the advancement of learning, by research into economic and political science, by education of the public therein, and by dissemination of ideas, research and the results of research in these subjects. The views expressed are those of the authors, not of the IEA, which has no corporate view.

Subscriptions

A subscription to the IEA Education and Training Unit ensures receipt of all the Unit's publications, as well as notices of seminars, conferences and special book offers. The Unit guarantees to publish at least 4 books per year. Special reduced rates are available for students and teachers. For more information write to the IEA Education and Training Unit at 2 Lord North Street, London SW1P 3LB.